JAN 7 1997

DATE DUE

Phil Simms on Passing

Phil Simms on Passing

Fundamentals of Throwing the Football

Phil Simms

with Rick Meier

WILLIAM MORROW AND COMPANY, INC.
NEW YORK

MEDWAY PUBLIC LIBRARY
26 HIGH STREET
MEDWAY MASS 02053

Copyright © 1996 by Phil Simms

Phil Simms game photographs: Jerry Pinkus, photographer, New York Football Giants; Dan Marino game photographs: Dave Cross, photographer, Miami Dolphins; Jim Kelly game photograph: Jim Bush, photographer, Buffalo Bills; John Elway game photograph: courtesy of the Denver Broncos
Physical training: Ronnie Barnes, head trainer, New York Football Giants, and Bill Parisi, Sports Conditioning Institute, Wyckoff, NJ
Anatomy and medical background: Steven J. McIlveen, MD, FACS, orthopedic surgeon, Sports Medicine, Valley Hospital, Ridgewood, NJ, and Lenox Hills Hospital, NY, NY

All rights reserved. No part of this book may be reproduced or utilized in any form or by any means, electronic or mechanical, including photocopying, recording, or by any information storage or retrieval system, without permission in writing from the Publisher. Inquiries should be addressed to Permissions Department, William Morrow and Company, Inc., 1350 Avenue of the Americas, New York, N.Y. 10019.

It is the policy of William Morrow and Company, Inc., and its imprints and affiliates, recognizing the importance of preserving what has been written, to print the books we publish on acid-free paper, and we exert our best efforts to that end.

Library of Congress Cataloging-in-Publication Data

Simms, Phil.
    Phil Simms on passing : fundamentals of throwing the football / by Phil Simms with Rick Meier.—1st ed.
        p.   cm.
    ISBN 0-688-14100-5
    1. Passing (Football)   I. Meier, Rick.   II. Title.
GV951.5.S54   1996
796.332′25—dc20
                                                    96-12904
                                                        CIP

Printed in the United States of America

First Edition

1 2 3 4 5 6 7 8 9 10

BOOK DESIGN BY INTERROBANG DESIGN STUDIO

One occasion will always stick in my mind, no matter how long I coach. It was my first day with the Giants, when I met Phil Simms. I remember right where we were standing, between the weight room and the coaches' offices. There I was, about to begin my first year in the pros . . . coaching a guy who had been a starter for thirteen years and a Super Bowl MVP. He'd already accomplished more in his career than I've ever dreamed of and I was supposed to teach him something.

As I recall, we shook hands and went through all the awkward preliminaries and then he asked me if I had seen any film of him. And I told him that I had. Then he asked me something that really set the tone for our relationship for the rest of the time I've known him: "Tell me what I need to do to improve." And I remember letting out the breath I'd been unconsciously holding, and launching into my philosophy on carrying the football in the pocket. After all he had accomplished, his biggest concern was how he could make himself better. And he kept asking me more questions—what I thought about this or that . . . and why. And he worked very hard at changing, breaking old habits, and making the fine adjustments that we thought would make the most of his natural ability and his skills. And I learned a lot from him, as I have from every other professional quarterback I've had the opportunity to work with since.

I think it gets back to something my high school coach told me a long time ago. He said, "You know, coaches have a fallacy, a misconception. They think they know it all." He told me that you have to get past that so you can really watch and listen to what your players tell you about what works and what doesn't—not just by what they say to you directly but by their performance. "If you can do that," he said, "you will continue to improve your effectiveness as a coach throughout your career." I've found that you can learn a lot from the people you're teaching. The more advanced the player, the better the feedback you'll get.

Phil and I have remained good friends over the years and we've continued to learn from each other. When he told me he was writing a book, there was no doubt in my mind that it would be thorough and comprehensive. I also knew that it would be rich in the values and work ethic that often bring out the best in all of us and elevate some to greatness.

–Jim Fassel
Offensive Coordinator and Quarterback Coach
Arizona Cardinals

ACKNOWLEDGMENTS

If I had to pick one person in particular who had a very significant impact on my career, it would Ron Ehrhardt. He was the offensive coordinator for the Giants under Bill Parcells and the man who removed the term "ya but" from my vocabulary, demanding nothing less than the best I could be.

The question from Ron was always, did you complete the pass or was it incomplete? There was no gray area. There was no "ya but, Coach, a 290-pound lineman got in my way. I couldn't throw the ten-yard out." Ron would say, "Ya but, ya but, ya but! We got a bunch of 'ya buts' today." He didn't want to hear that. His position was, if the receiver is open, throw him the football. Do something. Get yourself in position somehow and throw it to him. Get around the defensive lineman in your way. Throw the ball and complete the pass. The world was strictly yes or no, black or white with him when it came to my performance. And, I learned how to deal with the simple reality of that world. There was no middle ground.

It helped me immensely. It stripped away all of my alibis and it took all of the guesswork out of playing. Once I got over the fact that my feelings were going to get hurt more than I was probably used to, it was okay. There weren't any "ya buts" anymore. It's amazing when it gets that clear-cut, how you find ways to overcome the obstacles and get the job done. So, the guy was in my way. I had to anticipate that or throw blindly sometimes, knowing my receiver had to be there. I never had to sit around and ask myself, what do the coaches think or what do they want from me? I knew what they wanted. He communicated with me just fine. And that freed me up a lot and let me do whatever it took to win.

It's no accident that Ron's still out there on the sideline, running an offense that just happens to be having great success and a quarterback that went to the Super Bowl again. Time has shown that his methods work. You can see it in the records of the teams he coaches and the careers of the players he influences. They know how to win.

CONTENTS

A few seasons ago I was standing on the sidelines with a friend watching our sons play in a recreation league football game, and we were talking about the quality of the coaching the boys were getting, which we thought was very good. I made the comment that some of the best coaching I ever received hadn't come until well into my pro career. And he was amazed—not so much that I was still learning new techniques but that there were so few coaches around who could actually teach the mechanics that would help me play at a higher level. I told him that this late in my career, I was finding that I had to rely on sound fundamentals more than ever to be effective and play my best.

When I thought about it, my only regret was that I wasn't coached this way when I was in high school and college. I'm sure that's probably true for most of us in some way. Wouldn't it be great if you could go back to some important point in your life knowing what you know today? With the knowledge and maturity you've gained, there'd be no limit to what you could do.

It was during my thirteenth year as a pro that I had the good fortune to work with Jim Fassel, who was hired by the New York Giants in 1990 as our quarterback coach. Since then, he's gone on to coach for the Denver Broncos and the Oakland Raiders and most recently he was appointed offensive coordinator and quarterback coach for the Arizona Cardinals. Those two seasons with Jim were very important to me. They were like going back to junior high to learn the basic skills of my position all over again. He taught me not only the fundamentals of throwing the football, but also the reasons behind those techniques.

Before that time, when I'd struggle and things weren't going well, I'd try anything to improve my performance. I'd change my footwork, my grip on the ball, any number of things to help me increase my accuracy or my range. And sooner or later, I'd run across something that worked... and I would stay with it until the next slump came along. But it was a random thing. And I usually had no idea why any particular adjustment worked. It just did. When Jim Fassel took over, I started to understand the how and the why.

He was fortunate during his playing years to have had great coaching from the beginning: through high school, college, and the pros. And he'll tell you right away that his most important influence was Bill Walsh. Jim joined the coaching staff at Stanford the year after Bill Walsh left to coach the San Francisco 49ers, and for five years he worked within the system that Walsh created. Everybody in football knows the success that Coach Walsh enjoyed with the 49ers before he chose to return to college coaching at Stanford. Throughout his long and illustrious career Bill Walsh has earned the reputation as one of the true experts on quarterbacking and throwing the football. He's the one who really pioneered the scientific approach to teaching the position, breaking the action of throwing down to its most basic elements. Fassel bases a lot of his theories on the teachings of Coach Walsh. His experience at

Stanford was invaluable in formulating his offensive philosophies and his approach to working with quarterbacks.

His impact on my game has been immeasurable, not just in the skills I've refined and the techniques I've learned, but also in the sheer enjoyment I get from playing the game.

I'm proof positive that no matter how long you've been doing something, even if you're reasonably successful at it, you can learn to do it better. I guess old dogs *can* learn new tricks. What's even more important, though, is that young players now have the opportunity to build fundamentally sound throwing skills from the beginning, without the guesswork. Coaches can be more consistent and effective in their teachings. And quarterbacks at all levels can enjoy playing more at an earlier age because of their success on the playing field.

Good fundamental coaching has taken a lot of boys with average ability and turned them into good—and sometimes even great—high school and college quarterbacks, because they learned to apply every bit of talent they had and put it to work for themselves. And that's the objective of this book. What you will read and see in the pages ahead is a combination of what Jim taught me and the techniques I've learned on my own throughout my career. Our desire is to help players of all ages to maximize their natural throwing talents. The drills, the exercises, the illustrations, and the commentary are all tried-and-true stepping-stones to achieving that goal.

Watching my son throw the ball, I can see that he does things mechanically and fundamentally much better than I ever did when

HE TAUGHT ME TO WIN

Phil came from a small town in Kentucky and coming to New York can be very overpowering, especially for an athlete. He came here to step into the lead role as a quarterback of a pro team—and not just any team. He took over the most prestigious job in professional football, one of the top jobs in professional sports, the quarterback of the New York Giants. And the focus on that position is probably the toughest in professional sports. So, to come into New York without any experience in this market before, and to have to deal with all this media and all the people and the opinionated fans, was a real challenge. New York fans have got to be the toughest in pro sports.

His career as an athlete, as a professional quarterback, was always first. Even today, when we talk about other players who do meetings and promote themselves during the year and during the season, he can't fathom that. When it was football season, he concentrated totally on the season, on football. I think one of the big keys to his success is that he is so focused.

I was in college. And that's because I was able to help him learn a few important techniques as he was starting out. I tried to give him a good scientific foundation so that he wouldn't have to rely on guesswork when he tried to correct his mistakes. He enjoys throwing the football now because he knows, even at his young age, what he's doing and why it works.

Early success has helped him to build confidence and enjoy playing the game more. When I go out in the yard now and we toss

When he decides to take something on, he dedicates himself to it.

For a lot of players over the years, their contract was the big thing—their contract, their contract, their contract. Phil's philosophy as he expressed it to me was "Listen, I'm going take care of my stuff on the field. I'll load the gun. You shoot the bullets." The goal has always been very simple: be the best at what you can be and everything else, including the money, will come. People will acknowledge it. That's been his philosophy for years.

What was truly great about him from my point of view was that he taught me to win. He showed me that it's hard to lose. I've taken a lot from his business philosophy and a lot from his on-the-field philosophy and used it in my business. Be the best you can be and everything else will come.

There's no doubt in my mind that he'll always be a winner in whatever he does.

— David Fishof, David Fishof Presents
New York, New York

the ball around, I can see and understand what he's doing, right or wrong . . . and why. More important, *he* knows what he's doing and can correct his own mistakes. When I give him a pointer now and then, he understands what I'm talking about because we have a common language. We both know that what I'm telling him is sound and correct. And it's reassuring to know that what we're working on together is something he can build on for as long as he chooses to play the game. As a coach, parent, or player, that's all you can ask for.

Phil Simms on Passing

CHAPTER 1
Strong Fundamentals:
A Philosophy of Success

Figure 1.0 San Francisco, 1991. I've learned to carry the ball midchest with my arms and hands relaxed. My shoulders are parallel to the sidelines and I'm looking straight up the field.

Everyone feels the tension and the pressure of competition. The question is, Are you good enough to overcome it? What makes somebody a great clutch shooter in basketball? Why was Larry Bird so dependable on the free-throw line at the end of the game when everything was at stake? I'll tell you why. It was because he spent endless hours learning the fundamentals of shooting a basketball: practicing, shooting free throws after practice, working on his fundamentals, and refining his skills. He worked so hard and achieved such consistency that the outside forces could not overcome his ability to put the ball in the hole regardless of the situation.

I'm sure you've heard it said about a player after a poor game that he is normally good but the pressure got to him. The simple, hard truth is that if you're not good under pressure, you're probably not that good when there's no pressure. Athletes who can perform well under pressure don't lose their skills when the situation changes. Failure to perform under pressure—and I'm going to repeat this over and over again—means that you're not fundamentally sound enough to overcome any situation, no matter what sport you're playing.

Each time Larry Bird stepped up to the line in a clutch moment, he may have looked cool on the outside, but you can bet he felt the pressure inside. I'm sure his heart was racing and his stomach was turning.

But his shooting mechanics were so strong that even though he was nervous and feeling the stress of the situation, he could hit the shot. He'd done it over and over again in practice. And he could hit it again in the game, when it counted. The difference between Larry

Bird and most people is the time he spent in practice developing his strong fundamentals, learning how to shoot the basketball correctly and consistently. He'd worked so hard and so long that when he shot, his motion, release, and follow-through were automatic. Even though his insides were churning, he was equal to the challenge. Of course he was cool under pressure. He'd only made that shot a million times before, and he was good at it. The same is true with any reasonably talented athlete in any sport. The key to success is strong fundamentals.

So how do you get fundamentally sound? What does it mean? Number one, it means that you know and understand all the mechanics of the skill you're learning. In basketball the goal is putting the ball in the hoop. Doing that consistently from a number of positions on the court is the result of the way you hold the ball when you shoot; the position of your feet, your body, and your arms; and the follow-through of your hand as you release the ball.

In throwing the football, the goal is accuracy: hitting the receiver where he can catch the ball. The way you achieve that accuracy on a consistent basis is by learning the fundamentals of throwing that are unique to passing the football. There are other quarterbacking skills to learn, but right now all we're interested in is passing.

Learning and developing fundamental passing skills will make you a better passer. It will make you more consistently accurate. And it will help you to understand how to alter what you're doing in order to improve your performance. Knowing what you're doing physically and why it works removes all the guesswork.

strong fundamentals

SUCCESSFUL PASSERS TODAY

To be a successful quarterback today, first of all you have to be able to throw the football, which is not innate in every player. You need the ability to read and react properly to multiple situations. I think you have to respond positively to pressure and duress. You have to be able to throw the ball accurately. Phil's greatest characteristic as a passer was his accuracy. And I think you have to be able to anticipate changes and react almost before they happen. Other than that, you've got to be physically tough to withstand what's going to come your way, because it is going to come your way.

For younger players, I think it's very important to have someone there to assist them in some of the fundamentals that are necessary as well, if they want to move up from one level to the next. Even at the professional level, it's still important to have some-one there, even for the most proficient quarterbacks, to help remind the players of the skills and good habits that disappear from time to time—not so much to teach them a bunch of new things but more to steer them back to some of the important fundamen-tals when they need it.

—Bill Parcells
Former Head Coach, New York Giants
Head Coach, New England Patriots

It will also help you with the mental part of playing the position. As you experience success, I believe that your confidence will grow too. So will the confidence of your teammates. You'll know what you can do. You'll *know* that you can throw the football accurately every time because you understand the fundamentals and you've done it over and over again in practice.

In the pages ahead I'm going to show you how to throw the football and give you the drills and exercises you need to develop your fundamentals. The hard work and practice are up to you. The goal is consistency. When you throw a short-out to your left, you want to step, turn, set your feet, and rotate your hips and shoulders the same way, every time. You want to shift your weight, bend your knees, and release the ball with the same motion every time. That's how you gain confidence. That's how you win the confidence of people around you. That's how you learn to detach your physical performance from your emotions.

Maybe you won't become the next first-round draft pick of the Miami Dolphins, but that's okay. You may not lead a major college team to a national title, and that's okay too. Then again, you might. Who knows? What you will be able to do is use every bit of talent that the Good Lord gave you and put it all into play. Once you begin to improve your physical skills and feel your confidence grow, you'll find your leadership skills growing too. There's no mystery here. I became more of a leader with the Giants as I became more accomplished as a player. It became easier for me to lead by example. Everybody looks at you differently. They know what you've accomplished.

strong fundamentals

ROLE OF QB COACH

You expect a quarterback coach to address all the fundamental issues: the technical aspects of the game for the quarterback, the fundamentals, the mechanics, the reads, the choices, both the physical and the mental parts of the game as they pertain to each specific individual. You want to continue to work with your quarterbacks to help them stay on track fundamentally and develop themselves. Part of that developmental work is a certain amount of mental support in what they're doing too. You can't just throw a quarterback in, sink or swim, week after week. You support them when they're young and as they develop through high school and college and you keep on when they're in the pros. You have to continue that as long as they're playing. I know Phil needed that. I think you need to continue the support, the reinforcement, the reminders, all of those things as they go

I was a shy person in high school and in college. But I overcame a lot of that because of my performance as an athlete. It made me feel more confident as a person. And I think that happens to a lot of kids. It starts a little at a time. With a few good practices under your belt, you begin to feel better about yourself. And that feeling grows. Success breeds success. Coach pats you on the back and tells you to keep up the good work. Your game performance improves, and your teammates see that and respect you for it. You begin to conduct yourself differently off the field and in the classroom. Everything changes. Your whole life and personality change.

forward. I don't think you ever stop doing that. I also think eventually a quarterback has to have the ability to remind himself of things too, so that you work together to keep him on track and playing at his best.

A good coach has to be patient but adamant to the task. In other words, I think the quarterback position can get sidetracked with some unimportant accomplishment. You know, "He was 20 for 25, today... but, we lost. He did his part." Passing statistics are not his part. Percentages and numbers are not his job. The job is about getting your team into the end zone and winning, leading and not turning the ball over. Winning is the team's first goal in any game. The statistics of playing well are second.

–Bill Parcells
Former Head Coach, New York Giants
Head Coach, New England Patriots

strong fundamentals

I've always believed in setting high goals for myself. When you set your goals high, your work habits become more focused. You know why you're working hard. You want to start in the fall, or complete a certain number of passes—whatever makes sense to you. You need to have that goal, something that's important to you. It helps to keep you from thinking of your work as meaningless drudgery.

It's like an old story I heard a long time ago. Three men are working on the building site of a new cathedral, the largest in the world. A tourist walks by and asks one of the workers what he is doing. The worker tells him that he is digging this gigantic hole in the ground and complains about the grueling schedule. The man passes another worker and asks the same question. The second worker explains that he's getting paid ten dollars an hour to build this huge foundation and complains that the money is not enough. As the visitor turns to leave, he meets a third man whose attitude is considerably more positive. So he asks the third man what he's doing, and the worker tells him with pride and excitement that he's building the foundation of the largest, most beautiful cathedral in the world.

What do you see when you're working hard? I put in a lot of long hours in the off-season building my strength and refining my skills. But I never looked at it as torture. I might moan and groan a little when I work hard, but I always know what I'm reaching for.

Coaches—remember (especially with young players) that in addition to teaching your players the fundamental skills they'll need to excel at the sport, you must also show them that working hard can be fun. After all, they come to play because they enjoy the game. Help them to understand that the better they get, the more fun they can have. Plan your practices so that you keep your players moving. Vary your drills and present them in a positive light. Work them hard, but help them to keep in sight the goals they're laboring to achieve.

I remember one time I went to see my oldest son play baseball, and he got three hits. He was 3 for 3 that day and feeling pretty good about it. I asked him if he knew why he had done so well. He shrugged and talked about the pitches he was getting. I told him to think about all the hard work he had put in getting ready for that game, the hours he spent at the batting cage and on the soft toss. "You're enjoying the fruits of your labor," I said. "You've accomplished what you set out to do." I told him that he *should* feel good and to remember that feeling the next time he's struggling to achieve a goal.

Your day-to-day successes or failures do affect the way you see yourself. The extent depends on the individual. For me, building confidence and developing leadership qualities came from my success in athletics. And I never regret the effort and commitment it took to achieve those things. But all that didn't happen overnight. I didn't just wake up a leader one morning after a big game, full of confidence in what I could do. Confidence begins with the little things and it grows day by day: a step, a drop-back, a pass at a time. And it continues to grow over weeks, months, and years. Like the cathedral worker, you're building a foundation, block by block, skill by skill. It won't be easy. It's going to take a lot of hard work. But, if you keep a steady eye on what you're shooting for and honestly strive to get there, the results will be an achievement worth the effort.

strong fundamentals

CHAPTER 2
Warm-ups and Stretches

Figure 2.0   What's wrong with this picture? The overall form is good. My hips and shoulders are level and the ball is in the right position, but my left foot is out of position. It should be pointed more to the left, at my target. This kind of error will restrict my body rotation as I get toward the end of the throw.

Before stretching, before any specific warm-up exercises, you should always take two warm-up laps around the practice field or perform some other type of full-body exercise that will raise your core temperature and deliver blood to the legs, feet, arms, and fingers. Take your time. A slow jog is plenty. You're not trying to break a sweat. When you're done, your skin should just be slightly moist.

With those laps completed, you're ready for more specific warm-ups to prepare all the major muscle groups involved in running and throwing. Begin with some **jumping jacks.** Most of you have done these at some time in your athletic career. Begin by standing with your feet together and your hands at your sides. Jump and spread your feet so that when you land, they are shoulder width apart. At the same time raise your arms straight out from your sides over your head. As soon as you land in this position, jump again, bringing your hands back down to your sides and your feet back together. That's one jumping jack. Do fifty of them.

Figure 2.1a   **Figure 2.1b**

Follow them with ten **leg kicks** (Figure 2.1) with each leg. Make sure you're standing erect when you kick your leg forward with your knee straight. Complete the leg motion by swinging the leg back behind you as far as you can. The knee will naturally bend as you kick your leg backward in a pendulum-like motion. Do ten with one leg and then ten with the other.

Figure 2.2a

Figure 2.2b

Figure 2.2c

The other leg warm-up I like to do is the **side-to-side** (Figure 2.2). It's good for warming up the hamstrings, gluteals, and the calf muscles. Start by standing with your legs a little wider than

Figure 2.3a

Figure 2.3b

Figure 2.3c

Figure 2.3d

Figure 2.3e

warm-ups and stretches

Figure 2.4a   Figure 2.4b   Figure 2.4c

Figure 2.4d   Figure 2.4e

shoulder width apart, toes pointed slightly outward, knees slightly bent. Place your hands on your thighs just above your knees, and shift your weight, first to one leg and then the other. As you shift your weight to one side, that knee should bend while the opposite one straightens. You should feel a tug on the hamstring muscles in your straightened leg. Do twenty of these—ten each way.

One more warm-up exercise that includes the legs but also works on the torso and the upper body is the **squat thrust** (Figure 2.3). Begin by standing erect with your feet slightly apart, hands at your side. Then bend at your knees, and squat so that you can place your hands flat on the ground in front of you. In the same motion, kick both feet straight back so that you assume something like a push-up position. As soon as you land in this position, immediately push off your toes, and pull your knees up to get back in a squat position. Then stand up with your feet together and your hands at your side again. Do ten of these.

Figure 2.5a

Figure 2.5b

Figure 2.5c

Figure 2.5d

Next, we'll concentrate on the shoulders and upper arms by doing ten **large arm circles** (Figure 2.4). Extend your arms out from your sides as straight as you can, and begin rotating them forward so that your hands are tracing circles a foot or more in diameter. When you're finished, do ten rotations backward. Follow these with ten **small arm circles** (Figure 2.5) forward and ten backward, to concentrate your warm-up more on the finer musculature of the shoulder and rotator cuff. These circles shouldn't exceed a few inches in diameter.

We'll finish the warm-up with **trunk rotations** (Figure 2.6). Stand with your feet shoulder width apart, knees slightly bent, and hands on your hips. Now bend forward at the waist so that your trunk and head are parallel to the ground. Then rotate your trunk to one

warm-ups and stretches

Figure 2.6a

Figure 2.6b

Figure 2.6c

Figure 2.6d

side so that you can feel the pull on the opposite side. Continue your rotation around to the back. Lean back so that you can feel the tension in your abdominal muscles, and then rotate around to the other side. Again, you should feel tension in the muscles on the opposite side. Rotate forward again so that your trunk and body are parallel to the ground once more, and then stand up. Repeat this motion ten times each way. The complete warm-up should take about ten to twelve minutes to finish. Then you're ready to stretch. But remember, getting loose to throw the football means warming up not just the arm but the whole body, especially the legs.

WARM-UP SUMMARY
1. Fifty jumping jacks
2. Twenty leg kicks (ten per leg)
3. Twenty side-to-sides (ten per leg)
4. Ten squat thrusts
5. Twenty large arm circles (ten forward rotation; ten backward rotation)

6. Twenty small arm circles (ten forward rotation; ten backward rotation)
7. Twenty trunk rotations (ten starting to the left and ten starting right)

ARM WARM-UPS WITH MEDICINE BALLS

Jim Fassel has a whole series of medicine ball warm-ups that we used when he was with the Giants. One of them, the **chest pass**, is particularly effective because it not only warms up the hands, wrists, arms, and shoulders, but it also incorporates and reinforces some of the essential mechanics involved in throwing the ball.

Figure 2.7

Depending on your experience with them, most people think of medicine balls as big, heavy, and unwieldy—eight to ten pounds and fifteen inches or so in diameter. The balls I'm talking about can be as small as six inches in diameter and weigh a little over two pounds. They're usually made of soft plastic or rubber and come in a progression of weights, measured in metric standard or U.S.: two pounds, four pounds, six pounds, and so on (Figure 2.7).

The weight of the ball is very important, especially for younger players. You want to use enough weight to add resistance to the movement you're performing, but you don't want to alter the mechanics of it. Remember, you're just warming up, not building muscle mass. For example, young players—junior football into high school—shouldn't use a ball over 1 or 2 kilograms. That's 2.2. to 4.4 pounds. Make sure you look to see in which standard the ball is weighed. A metric kilogram is equivalent to 2.2

| Figure 2.8a | Figure 2.8b | Figure 2.8c |

pounds. So a ball marked as 3 kilograms actually weighs about 6.6 pounds. When in doubt, work light.

When you're doing the **chest pass** (Figure 2.8) warm-up with a medicine ball, you'll need a partner. Stand facing each other about five yards apart (closer for younger children if they're straining to make the throw). Hold the ball chest high, hands at the sides of the ball. Your feet should be shoulder width apart. As you chest pass the ball to your partner, you should step forward with your throwing leg: that's your left leg if you throw right-handed and the right for lefties. Step forward in a normal stride so that your foot lands heel to toe as you release the ball. Your knee should bend slightly as your weight shifts from your back foot to the front foot. As you release the ball, you should rotate your thumbs downward, in a motion similar to your release motion as you throw the football. Step and throw the ball from your chest with both hands, rotating your thumbs downward, with a snap as you release.

The step is a very important part of this drill. Landing heel to toe so that your knee naturally bends is an essential component of your throwing motion with the football. Landing toe-first naturally tends to lock out your knee so that you land straight-legged. This limits your ability to complete the rest of your throwing motion and puts more strain on your arm. We'll cover the complete mechanics of throwing in a later chapter; for now, concentrate on landing heel-toe and snapping the thumbs downward when you release the medicine ball.

STRETCHES

The main difference between warming up and stretching is the lack of motion in stretching. Each time you stretch some portion of your body, you should reach the point where you feel a tug (not pain) on the muscles involved and then hold for eight to ten seconds. Remember, no bouncing. Just stretch to the point of pressure without pain and hold.

Figure 2.9

Begin with a **standing leg stretch** (Figure 2.9). Knees straight, bend at the waist and grab your ankles. You should feel tension but no pain in the hamstring muscles in the back of your thigh. Hold this position for eight to ten seconds.

Figure 2.10a   **Figure 2.10b**

In another variation of the standing leg stretch that some people call a **right-over-left leg stretch** (Figure 2.10), you cross your legs, right over left, and grab your ankles. Remember again to keep your knees straight and hold for eight to ten seconds.

warm-ups and stretches

Then switch so your left leg is over your right and repeat the stretch for eight to ten seconds. Again, these are very effective for the hamstrings and lower back.

Figure 2.11a   Figure 2.11b

The other important upper leg stretch is the **groin stretch** (Figure 2.11). Start by sitting on the ground with your feet in front of you. Spread your legs and bend your knees, bringing your feet together in front of you. Grab hold of your feet and pull them toward you. You should feel tension in the groin area and the inside of your thighs without any pain. Hold this position for eight to ten seconds.

Arm and Shoulder

Effective stretching of the forearm, arm, and shoulder muscles is particularly important for quarterbacks before they start to throw the ball. Remember, a loose muscle is an efficient muscle. Warming up and stretching the arm and shoulder muscles enable you to complete the motion of throwing the ball with all the proper mechanics. These warm-ups prepare the relevant muscles and joints for their job. They help to prevent injury and soreness. Throwing without warming up can cause injury by forcing you to alter your normal mechanics to compensate for a lack of flexibility. Remember also that you should always warm up and stretch both arms, not just your throwing arm. Both arms should go through the same routine.

Figure 2.12a

Figure 2.12b

Figure 2.12c

Begin with **forearm stretches** (Figure 2.12). Extend your arm out in front of you, with your palm up. Now reach over with the opposite hand, grab your fingers, and pull them down toward the floor so that your elbow straightens and your wrist bends backward (Figure 2.12a).

You should feel tension in the muscles between your elbow and your wrist. Hold this position for about ten seconds. With your arm still extended in front of you, turn your hand over so the palm faces the floor, and push the back side of your hand down, bending your wrist toward your body while straightening your elbow (Figure 2.12b). This time, you will feel tension in the muscles on the back of your forearm. If it hurts, you're pushing too hard. Back off so you just feel the muscles tug, and hold this position for eight to ten seconds.

Now, with your arm in the same position, palm down, straighten your elbow and pull your fingers upward and back toward your body with the opposite hand (Figure 2.12c). Hold this for eight to ten seconds and remember to repeat this same routine with the other arm before you go on to the next stretch.

warm-ups and stretches

Figure 2.13

Figure 2.14

The next set of exercises are designed to stretch the shoulder muscles and the muscles of the upper arm. For these, you'll need a four- to five-foot length of broom handle or a bath towel. We'll demonstrate with a broom handle but either works just as well. Begin the **front shoulder stretch** (Figure 2.13) by grabbing the handle at both ends (a little more than shoulder width apart) and hold it out in front of you at shoulder level. The elbows should be slightly bent. Pull at both ends of the handle with equal pressure at both ends for eight to ten seconds. You should feel the effects in front of your shoulders. Now raise your arms over your head, still holding the handle at both ends, and pull again for the full eight to ten seconds. Notice that the tug this time has shifted to the back of the shoulder. So we'll call this one the **back shoulder stretch** (Figure 2.14).

Figure 2.15a

Figure 2.15b

Another variation of the towel or broom-handle stretch targets the triceps muscles on the backside of the upper arm (Figure 2.15). This time raise your throwing hand up over your head while holding on to one end of the handle, allowing the other end to fall behind your back.

Grab the loose end behind your back with your free hand. The idea here is to pull down on the handle with your hand behind your back while resisting with the hand over your head. Hold the **triceps stretch** for eight to ten seconds and release. Remember, if you feel pain, you're pulling too hard. Be sure to repeat the same stretch with your nonthrowing arm.

The rotator group of muscles in the shoulder (see Chapter 7, Figure 7.6) is one of the most important components of your throwing motion. These muscles support the shoulder joint, and it's easy to injure them in the act of throwing if they're not properly warmed up and stretched.

Figure 2.16a

Figure 2.16b

One of the best stretching exercises I know for the rotators also makes use of a towel or a broom handle. Begin the **forward rotator stretch** (Figure 2.16) by raising your throwing hand, palm forward, as if you were pledging allegiance. Your arm should be bent at the elbow in a L shape, upper arm parallel to the floor. Place one end of the handle in your raised hand, allowing the other end to fall back over the back side of the arm. Then reach across your body with your other hand and grab the loose end of the handle. Holding on to both ends of the handle this way, push up on the handle with your front hand while resisting with the raised hand. Hold for about eight to ten seconds. Again—no pain. Repeat this stretch using the other hand.

warm-ups and stretches

Together, these three exercises make up a very effective internal and external rotation stretch you can do by yourself for all the large muscles in the upper arm and shoulder, including the biceps and triceps.

Figure 2.17

The last rotator stretch that I like to use requires a partner. In this **two-person rotator stretch** (Figure 2.17), the player stretching stands with his feet a comfortable distance apart, and his arms straight out from his sides, palms forward. His partner stands behind him, close enough so he can take hold of the stretcher's wrists and pull them back slowly until the person stretching feels the muscles in the front part of his shoulders tugging without pain. Hold for eight to ten seconds.

Having completed the full regimen of warm-ups and stretches, the muscles in your arms, trunk, and legs should be loose. You should be ready to throw. Remember, you want elastic muscles and a full range of motion for optimal power, velocity, and control of the ball.

STRETCH SUMMARY
(hold each for eight to ten seconds)
1. Standing leg stretch
2. Right-over-left leg stretch
3. Groin stretch
4. Forearm stretches
5. Towel/broom-handle series—shoulder and upper arm
6. Two-person rotator stretch

Figure 3.0   Hands in good position, thumb side to thumb side, and I've got my head up looking downfield. Remember, good execution at the snap is like getting a good start in a race.

THE STANCE

Taking the snap from the center is typically one of those critical little skills that you cover the first day of junior football practice and is subsequently neglected. As long as you get the ball and hold on to it, there's not much to say. Right? How difficult can it be? Well, like most things that look simple, the key to consistent performance lies in the fine details. It's *not* a complex thing to do. But successfully taking the snap does depend on whether or not you do a lot of little things right, the same way every time, beginning with the position of your feet as you prepare to receive the ball. I've always thought that standing under center, waiting for the snap of the ball, was a lot like being a runner at the starting line just before the gun sounds the start of the race. You want to be in just the right position with your feet and body so you can get off to a good start. A bad stance forces you to play catch-up the rest of the way. It can throw everyone's timing off and put you at a decided disadvantage.

Pigeon-toed

One of the first things Jim Fassel wanted to change in my technique was the position of my feet as I took the snap from Bart Oates, who was the New York Giants' center at the time. He was trying to eliminate an extra step I was taking as I started to drop back to pass. This flaw wasn't unique to me. Most quarterbacks do it.

As they receive the ball, many right-handed quarterbacks will lift their left foot and reposition it so they can pivot and push off to take their first step away from center with their right. That first lifting of the left foot is wasted movement that costs time. You should be able to make that move in one step. Remember, as I said in the

DROPPED SNAPS

It's never just one person's fault when you fail to complete a snap from center. The two of you have to work together. You would think that as the most basic, most fundamental part of the game, the center snap to the quarterback would be routine. And it is for the most part. But, particularly in the heat of the battle, when the center is under a lot of pressure from a defensive player, you sometimes have the tendency to change things slightly. And even a slight change in the delivery of the football can and does cause a bad snap and a fumble. Once you both have the correct fundamentals down, the rest takes practice and game experience. You should make it a habit to go out before practice and work just on the center snap. We did that in camp and we did it all year long. It became a fixture, a five-minute session we did just about every day.

—Bart Oates
Center, San Francisco 49ers

Figure 3.1

beginning, we want to get off to a good start so we're not rushing to catch up.

Jim's solution to the extra-step problem calls for the quarterback to stand under center with his toes turned slightly inward, in a pigeon-toed stance (Figure 3.1). It's not a natural thing to do for most people, and it's easy to forget in the fray of the

the basics

27

game. But it's one of those little habits that adds efficiency and is well worth acquiring.

Figure 3.2

The pigeon-toed stance puts your feet in a better position to move as you open to drop back, roll out, or turn to hand the ball off. It tends to shift your weight so it's concentrated more on the inside edge of the ball of your foot (Figure 3.2). With your weight in this position, you're almost forced to rotate your heel outward quickly and push off your left foot on the ball of the foot as you step with your right. You don't have to false-step anymore because your foot is ready to pivot before you start. A left-handed passer, pivoting on his right foot, enjoys the same advantage since the technique calls for both feet to be turned slightly inward.

Figure 3.3a

Figure 3.3b

Feel the Difference

So you can really feel the difference, try taking the snap with your toes straight ahead. Get in your stance as if you were behind the center, and make your first step to drop back. Remember, this step should be as perpendicular to the line of scrimmage as you can make it. You want to go straight back on your drops. That means that you're going to have to open your hips pretty wide to get that far around (Figure 3.3). In order to make that first step with your feet straight, you first have to shift your weight to the inside

FALSE-STEPPING: I had the opportunity to speak with the quarterback coach of the Kansas City Chiefs, Paul Hackett, who's a big-time disciple of Bill Walsh. He said that when he went to Kansas City, he worked with Joe Montana and David Craig. Paul told me that when he started working with Dave Craig in the off-season it was almost two weeks before he would let him throw one football. He said that Craig had a false step. He'd pick his left foot up and reset it before he'd come back with his first drop-step. Paul told me he could never understand why you would want to take two steps to get off the line when you should be taking one. It took him forever to break the habit. Craig said that nobody had ever told him that before. Paul told him, "Well, you know it now." He said that David would beg him to let him throw a football. But Paul told him, "Not until you're ready." And he just kept him working till he finally broke the habit. I always false-stepped before Jim worked with me. Like Dave Craig, I never realized it was a problem. But once I learned not to do it, I figured out how much easier, smoother, and quicker my drops could be if I didn't take two steps in the time I should have been taking one. I never claimed it would be easy to break old habits. I just said it was possible with enough motivation and the right instruction.

—P.S.

the basics

edge of your left foot and then rotate the heel about eight to ten inches outward. The instinctive thing to do is lift your foot and reposition it.

BAD HABITS: I was announcing a pro game one Sunday, and the guys in the booth told me to watch very closely a tape of one of the quarterbacks. They said that every time he intended to throw the football, he set his right foot in a distinct position. I thought they were ribbing me. But I watched and it was true. He did it almost every time. When he got into this one position, he threw the football. Of course, his coaches realized it too, and they corrected it before his next opponent could take advantage of it. I'm sure if we knew about it, his next opponent did as well. A fundamentally sound stance—pigeon-toed, level hips and shoulders, head up and looking down-field—won't give away anything and it gets you off the line of scrimmage as efficiently as possible.

—P.S.

Figure 3.4a

Figure 3.4b

Figure 3.4c

Now make the same move starting from a pigeon-toed stance. Don't turn your toes in too much—just slightly, so you can feel your weight shift to the inside edge of the balls of your feet (Figure 3.4). Now, as you step away, the heel naturally pivots out, and you can really propel yourself back, away from the line of scrimmage.

PUSHING TOO HARD: When I was in high school and college, I used to put a lot of pressure against the center with my top hand when I took the snap. I'd push so hard, sometimes I almost pushed him over. When you do that, you get tremendous separation of your hands when the ball is snapped. I'm sure that's one of the reasons that Bart Oates and I fumbled so many times in 1985—I was generating so much pressure on Bart with my top hand that even though the snap would be right where it should be, my hand would come apart with the impact of the ball. I couldn't close on it. But think about it a minute: When you push that way, you're pushing upward with your top hand, away from the bottom one. When the center snaps it, the ball slams against a more rigid top hand that is pulling away from the bottom hand. The bottom hand can't catch up, and you get a gap between the two hands that the ball can squirt through—especially if it's snapped hard. The other thing that too much top-hand pressure can do is throw the center off balance. The upward pressure forces him forward and makes it harder for him to get the ball where it belongs and to make his block. And let me tell you— you don't want to make it more difficult for the linemen to make their blocks.

—P.S.

the basics

> **PUSHING TOO HARD: Sometimes, at the snap, Phil would push harder. A lot of quarterbacks do that. It makes your job at center a lot more difficult when a quarterback puts a lot of forward pressure on you, particularly on a pass when you're trying to get back off the ball and he's pushing you forward. If you've got a guy on the line of scrimmage across from the guard and you've got to slide over and get in front of him, that creates an extreme hardship when you have an angle like that to overcome. You've only got so many different angles. You have a nose tackle that you have to block. He may play off of you a little bit sometimes or he may play right on you. If the defensive tackles play right over the guards, you may be responsible for sliding over to block one of them in combination with the guard. So you've got to be able to get off the mark quickly once the quarterback has the ball. Pushing the center off balance adds at least one more step to that move and increases the risk of him not getting there in time.**
>
> **—Bart Oates**
> **Center, San Francisco 49ers**

You've got much better leverage, and you can move in one fluid motion. You've actually eliminated two steps. In the pigeon-toed stance, your weight is already over the inside ball of your foot, and you've started the rotation of your heel outward. Now, when you step out with your right foot to drop, your hips open easily and you're on your way. It's a little thing, but how often does an extra second in the course of a game mean the difference between a completed pass and a sack?

Figure 3.5a   Figure 3.5b

Shoulder Width

Another small point to remember is not to make your stance too wide. Shoulder width is plenty (see Figure 3.4a). You want your feet under you for balance and your weight off of your heels and over the balls of your feet for mobility. Try this: Stand with your feet shoulder width apart and lock your knees out (Figure 3.5a). You should feel your weight evenly distributed across both feet. Now bend your knees a little and feel the weight come off of your heels and onto the balls of your feet—just enough so that you feel balanced and mobile (Figure 3.5b). That's the way you should feel as you take the snap.

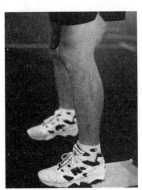

Figure 3.6a   Figure 3.6b

The Paper Test

A good test to see if you're in the correct position is to try the same thing on a bare wood floor, with your tennis shoes on (Figure 3.6). Put a sheet of paper under the heels of both shoes, and then assume your stance under center. Now, ask your buddy to remove the paper. It should just barely slide out without tearing. Be sure your heels are only slightly off the floor. The paper should come out easily enough, but you should not be able to slide it back under the shoe.

the basics

BOTTOM-HAND PRESSURE

Most fumbled snaps happen because the quarterback's hands get separated during the center/quarterback exchange, and the ball pops through. I know, because it was one of the problems I had early in my career. Hand position is probably the most critical detail in taking the ball from the center and the one that gives younger players the most trouble. Because their hands tend to separate, the shock of the snap hits the top hand, and they lose control of the ball. With good hand position and effective bottom-hand pressure, even the youngest player can learn to hold on to the ball consistently.

Figure 3.7

Thumb Side to Thumb Side

When you place your hands under the center, begin by putting the back of your throwing hand under him, fingers spread comfortably, with your middle finger at the midline (Figure 3.7). Now take your other hand, fingers spread, and place it next to the other, thumb side against thumb side. Your top hand should be relaxed but firmly in place. And the fingers of your bottom hand should point downward, with the palm forward.

One of the most important elements in receiving and controlling the ball is the position of your bottom arm, especially the elbow. With your hands in the correct position, straighten out the elbow of your bottom hand. This will bring your elbow in and underneath your top arm. At first, this position may seem uncomfortable. Be patient. You'll get used to it, especially when you feel how securely you can take the snap.

Figure 3.8a **Figure 3.8b**

The action between your hands in this position does two things. Because your top hand is relaxed, it absorbs the shock of the snap (Figure 3.8). The bottom hand closes tightly on the ball from the bottom up (bottom-hand pressure). The top hand is loose while the bottom is ready to snap closed under the ball. The feeling of this position is an easy way to remember that you're doing it the right way.

Now, with your hands in position, looking over the center, downfield, make sure that you lean forward slightly, with your back fairly erect. Keep your head up, chin out, and your shoulders back so you can see clearly up and down the line and into the defensive secondary (Figure 3.9). Now you're ready to get off to a good start.

Figure 3.9

Two Hands

Next time you see a college or a NFL quarterback fumble the ball while he's moving in the pocket, watch the instant replay and pay particular attention to the way he's carrying the ball. Nine times out of ten I'll bet he's carrying the ball in one hand, away from his body (Figure 3.10). How to avoid fumbles? Keep the ball close to your body, and use both hands (Figure 3.12). It's really that simple. That's the only way I know of to keep the ball from get-

the basics

Figure 3.10   At home against the 49ers, 1984. What's wrong with this picture? I'm back in the pocket looking for someone to break loose. The problem is that my hands are separated. During my last three years I never worked in the pocket without both hands on the ball—and I never fumbled.

ting knocked loose by an attacking lineman. It also has a tendency to keep you more relaxed and fluid as you move. Done correctly, it will also shorten the motion of throwing. (For simplicity, I'll describe the technique for a right-handed passer. If you're a lefty like my son, reverse the descriptions.)

Figure 3.11a   **Figure 3.11b**

After you take the snap, bring the ball up with both hands to the center of your body, chest high. The points of the ball should be vertical. Your elbows should be in and the ball close to your body but not touching (Figure 3.11a). Moving with your elbows out creates a pendulum effect that sways the ball from side to side (Figure 3.11b). You want to carry the ball smoothly, with very little motion away from the center of your body.

As an experiment, try running with the ball in both hands with your elbows out. The natural motion of running will cause the ball to shift back and forth across your chest. Now pull your elbows in and try it again. Keep your arms and shoulders loose. You'll find that the ball doesn't move nearly as much and that it's harder for a passing defender to hit.

You can really feel the difference in your shoulders. With your elbows in, your whole upper body is more relaxed. You're loose and balanced. When you extend your elbows outward, you can feel your chest and shoulder muscles tighten up. Remember, you

the basics

FUMBLES: When I look back at all the fumbles I had in my career, I realize that they were due to a really bad habit of taking one hand off the ball when I was flushed out of the pocket or even when I was just standing there getting ready to throw. I'd pull one hand off the ball. I grew up doing it. A lot of quarterbacks did. It wasn't even a conscious decision. It just happened. The problem was, the defense would slap the ball out of my hands every once in a while. Worse yet, I'd sometimes lose it when I was tackled. Even the slightest hit would jar the ball loose if I wasn't expecting it. It wasn't until my thirteenth year in the league that I broke that habit: Jim taught me to keep both hands on the ball. The effect was remarkable. Over those last three years I never fumbled the football again—not once. I still got hit a lot: moving in the pocket, running for my life, guys swiping at the ball, blind hits and all. I never coughed it up again because I learned to keep two hands on the ball. In fact, after Dan Reeves took over the Giants, I noticed once, when we were looking at game films, that my hands separated as I was dropping back, and I pointed it out. From that point on the coaches worked very hard with all the quarterbacks to keep us from doing that. And it helped a lot to cut down our team turnovers for the year.

—P.S

Figure 3.12   Good drop mechanics: On my second step from center, a crossover step, my shoulders are parallel to the sideline, the ball is chest high and in both hands, and I'm looking up the field. Look at the hands. My grip on the ball is so relaxed at this latter point in my career that you can barely see the bones in my hand.

the basics

Figure 3.13a

Figure 3.13b

Figure 3.13c

Figure 3.13d

never want tight muscles when you're trying to throw the football.

Front-Hand Pressure

In addition to keeping your elbows in, you can reduce ball movement even further during the drop by applying a little pressure with your front hand against the natural sway of the ball. Jim Fassel calls it **front-hand pressure** (Figure 3.13). As you drop back from the line to pass, you should try to hold the football so that you're exerting pressure on it with your front hand, pushing the ball back against your natural tendency to sway as you move. Continuing the same pressure as you stop will naturally move the ball into throwing position. Front-hand pressure moves the ball into position so you can easily cock your arm to throw. The term **front-hand pressure** helps me to remember the feeling I want as I move with the ball and prepare to throw. We'll talk about it again in Chapter 5 when we begin to cover the details of throwing the ball.

DROPPING BACK TO PASS

Most drop-back passing is done from a three-, five-, or seven-step motion away from the line of scrimmage. Generally, the more time

the basics

> **BLOCKING:** The offensive line knows where the quarterback should be on certain plays. And the timing. With Phil, you never really knew because he seemed to be oblivious to the physical punishment. He would hold on to the ball, not really concerned that he was going to take a big shot. He would wait for something to open up. So as his offensive linemen, you always prepared for the worst-case scenario. You figured that you were going to have to control your opponent for four or five seconds.
>
> **—Bart Oates**
> **Center, San Francisco 49ers**

you need to get the ball off, the more steps you want to take before you throw. More specifically, you'll use three- and five-step drops (90 percent of the time) to throw "timing" routes, patterns in which the ball is delivered to a specific spot on the field in a specific amount of time. You should also use the five-step drop when you throw long. Typically, seven-step drops are used for "maneuver routes," patterns where the receiver has options to beat the defense. Here you need more depth from the line and time for the receiver to get open.

Three-Step
The three-step drop (Figure 3.14) is ideal for quick outs, slants, and three- to five-yard curl or hitch routes. The idea here is to drop back and deliver the ball to your target in a set time and rhythm. These are the ultimate timing routes.

Figure 3.14a

Figure 3.14b

Figure 3.14c

Figure 3.14d

Figure 3.14e

As you position yourself under center, think pigeon-toed, balls of your feet, bottom-hand pressure, pivot, step, and two hands. When you receive the ball and begin to drop, you want your shoulders over your hips so that your feet initiate all the movement. Smoothness and timing are the keys.

Bring the ball up to your chest as you pivot, open your hips, and take your first full step back with your right foot. Try to make that first step as perpendicular to the line of scrimmage as you can, straight back from center. Remember, as you drop, your shoulder should be perpendicular to the line of scrimmage and your head should be erect, looking toward the defense and your receivers.

Your second step in a three-step drop is a crossover step; left foot over right, followed by another extended step with your right foot. When your right foot lands, you don't want the heel to touch the ground because you want to be able to pivot on your back foot as you step with your front foot to throw, either right or left. In fact (and we'll talk about this more in the next chapter), as you land on the last step, you should actually start the throwing motion. It is wasted motion to land flat-footed and then rise up on the ball of your foot so you can pivot, step, and throw.

Another thing you must accomplish as you drop back for a three-step drop is to land on the third and final step with your weight on the inside of your right foot and the inside of the knee. This way, when you land, you have the leverage to start the throwing motion immediately. Your weight will be in the ideal position to push off from your right foot and propel your body forward in the direction you want to throw.

Let's look at it one more time (Figure 3.15). In a three-step drop, you take your first step away from center with your right foot, so it lands perpendicular to the line of scrimmage. The second step is a short crossover. Third, reach back with your right foot so that it hits the ground with the heel slightly off the ground so you can pivot to where you want to throw the ball. Remember, the most important thing about the three-step drop is that you want to be able to throw the ball immediately. So when the right foot lands, you must have your weight on the inside of your right knee and the inside of the ball of your right foot so you have the leverage to propel yourself forward to throw with accuracy and ease. Your right foot and leg should be like a spring. When the back leg hits, you should be coming forward to throw the football. The rhythm is one, two, three, and throw.

the basics

Figure 3.15a   Figure 3.15b   Figure 3.15c

Figure 3.15d   Figure 3.15e

One more quick point here. You know what kind of routes your receivers are running. You know where they're supposed to be when you land. So, as you step away from the line of scrimmage on your first step, you should be looking downfield at the overall situation. On the second step, the crossover step, you should look to the area where you want to throw the ball, because on the third step you should be throwing.

Finally, take your time as you begin. Rhythm, smoothness, and consistency are more important than speed. Get it right by starting out very slowly and the speed will come as you practice.

DON'T RUSH IT: My problem with slipping started with the violent way I ran my drops sometimes, trying to get back in the pocket as fast as I could. When I think about it now, I don't really know why I was in such a hurry. Nobody was ever ready to catch that ball when I got there. It happened most frequently on seven-step drops, when I had receivers running longer patterns or maneuver routes or something of that order. So I was breaking my neck trying to get back there to set up and throw to a person who wasn't ready and wouldn't be for a couple of seconds. I'd look and my receivers would still be running the first leg of their routes.

When I raced back that hard, I'd have to be just as violent in trying to stop myself. So I would lean forward. Then I'd be off balance. And that's how the slipping would begin. It was a common thing for me. I can't tell you how many times I slipped when I did that. But I do remember a couple of times when I actually threw for touchdowns because of the slipping. I had fallen and I guess the defense thought I was down for good. But I got back up and—boom!—there was a receiver downfield with nobody covering him. It was a situation where two wrongs didn't make a right but they were good enough for six points.

—P.S.

the basics

Five-Step

This time you step, cross over, step, cross over, step, and throw (Figure 3.16). Again, you want to land on that final step with your weight on the inside of your right foot and pressure on the inside

Figure 3.16a   Figure 3.16b   Figure 3.16c

Figure 3.16d   Figure 3.16e   Figure 3.16f

of the right knee so you're in a position to propel yourself toward the target and throw. You don't want your weight to get to the outside of your right foot as you plant your last step. Think about it: If you don't fall over, you've got to work twice as hard to get your momentum shifted forward again. You almost have to re-gather yourself to get the weight on the inside of your foot again so you can throw. And that's the kind of wasted motion that we've been trying to avoid. It throws off the rhythm of the three- and five-step drop.

Seven-Step

The seven-step drop (Figure 3.17) is different from the other two because it involves three running steps and four quick drop steps. More specifically, when you receive the ball, you rotate and step

Figure 3.17a

Figure 3.17b

Figure 3.17c

Figure 3.17d

Figure 3.17e

Figure 3.17f

Figure 3.17g

Figure 3.17h

Figure 3.17i

the basics

Figure 3.18a

Figure 3.18b

Figure 3.18c

Figure 3.18d

Remember, on the first three steps of a seven-step drop, turn your back to the line of scrimmage. Make your first step perpendicular to the line and make three good strides to put distance between you and the defense.

as you did before, but instead of keeping your front shoulder downfield, let it turn away from the line of scrimmage. Your hip and shoulder both turn away. Turn and run back—three big steps. But remember to keep your head in a position that allows you to look over your shoulder and see downfield.

On the fourth step, which is the first quick step, your front shoulder should return to its downfield position, which is perpendicular to the line of scrimmage. This is your first crossover step. Don't rush it. Stay under control, with your body centered. You cross over (left over right), then step with your right, cross over (left over right) again, and then land with your right foot on step seven. Step seven is your extension step. Again, don't overextend this last step by leaning forward as you land to try to stop yourself, or you may slip and fall.

Once more—when you do a seven-step drop, you take three running steps away from the line. When you land on the third step, you cross over on the fourth, step on the fifth, cross over on the sixth, and land with the right foot on the seventh. Take your time as you begin to work on the seven-step drop, and walk through it. Speed and rhythm will come as you get used to what you're doing.

Slipping

Sometimes you'll see a quarterback slip on a wet field as he lands on that last step. If you're watching the game on television, look closely at the instant replay. You'll probably see him overextend the last step and lean forward with his body to try to stop himself on the slippery surface. When I say "overextend," I mean that his back foot has landed outside the plane of his back shoulder. That's something you want to avoid. Keeping your shoulders over your hips and your weight centered as you move will usually solve the problem of slipping and allow you to get the ball off more quickly. The big thing is to keep yourself under control and centered. Don't rush. Stay level, with your shoulders over your hips, in position to throw.

Slide-and-Gather

The most important difference between the seven-step drop and the others is that it's intended for maneuver routes, not timing patterns. Your receiver will be running farther down the field, to open areas of the defense. The same is true for the five, if you're throwing long. In these situations, when you land on the last step, you

the basics

Figure 3.19a

Figure 3.19b

Figure 3.19c

Figure 3.19d

Figure 3.19e

probably won't plant and throw immediately. First, you'll take what I used to call a hitch step, forward. For our purposes here, we'll call it the **slide-and-gather** step (Figure 3.19). It's a step back toward the target to help you gain enough momentum and leverage to propel the ball farther down the field.

As you plant your right foot on the seventh step, you should still land as you did before, with your weight on the inside of the knee and ball of the foot. But this time you should take a slide step forward with your front foot, shifting your weight forward momentarily, while you gather your back foot under yourself again. As you move that back foot into position, you want to re-

Figure 3.20a

Figure 3.20b

Figure 3.20c

Figure 3.20d

Figure 3.20e

Figure 3.20f

Figure 3.20g

Figure 3.20h

Figure 3.20i

the basics

Notice the way I land on the ball of my back foot and rotate my heel slightly inward (3.20b). It's a little thing but it makes it easier to slide-and-gather to my right before I throw the football.

MOBILITY IN THE POCKET: I jumped a lot of rope when I was a kid. My dad told me that I needed to have quick feet. And that's one attribute I think I've always had. I'm not fast as far as the forty-yard dash is concerned, but when I'm in the pocket, one of the best things I'm able to do is move quickly and still be in position to throw the ball. I can make someone miss me and still have enough vision downfield to make a decision and throw the football. That came with practice and experience being in the pocket, from dropping back and throwing the football a lot. If sometimes I get sloppy in my passing, for me it's not because of my arm technique. Usually it's my footwork. If I'm off balance when I throw, it's because I'm not getting my whole body in position to throw the football.

–Dan Marino
Quarterback, Miami Dolphins

establish your weight on the inside portion of it so you can push off and throw.

It's almost like a crow step in baseball. Young players learn to do it to throw the ball in from the outfield or to make the long throw from third to first. It allows you to put more of your body behind the ball and get more power into the throw.

Just to review it again: As you land on the fifth or seventh step during a drop, the weight should be on the inside portion of your right foot and lower leg, just as it was when you were throwing the three-step drop. But this time, instead of throwing right away,

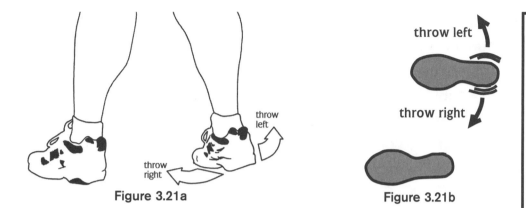

Figure 3.21a   Figure 3.21b

On the last step of your drop, land with your weight concentrated on the inside portion of your foot with your heel slightly off the ground. A right-handed passer who is throwing to his left should land so his heel is rotated slightly outward. This will make it easier to pivot on your back foot and open your hips in the direction of the throw. When you throw right, rotate the heel slightly to the inside.

you're going to take a slide-and-gather step back toward the line of scrimmage and the receiver before you throw.

You're going to land on your right foot and slide your left foot forward, shifting your weight briefly as you do, so you can gather your right leg under yourself again, to push off and throw. Remember to point the toe of your front foot toward the target when you slide (Figure 3.20).

Again, the reason you're taking this extra step back toward the receiver is so you can really propel yourself forward. The object is to get all of your weight—your hips and shoulders—over to your front foot as you throw the football.

THROWING RIGHT OR LEFT
So far, everything we've talked about describes passes thrown straight down the field. When you're throwing right or left off of

the basics

a three- or five-step drop, one of the fine details that will help you to be a little more efficient involves the angle of your back foot as you land to throw. A right-handed passer throwing to his left should land on his back foot with his heel just off the ground and rotated slightly outward. This makes it easier to pivot on the back foot and opens the hips in the direction of the throw. When you throw right, rotate the heel of your back foot more to the inside (Figure 3.21).

Aside from landing with your weight on the inside, you don't have to worry about the angle of your back foot on the five- or seven-step drop to throw long, because you will adjust your feet again toward the receiver as you take your slide-and-gather step.

We'll cover the details of throwing right and left in a later chapter, after we've described the fundamentals of throwing the football.

POINTS TO REMEMBER
- On the three- and five-step drops, you always want to keep your shoulders perpendicular to the line of scrimmage.
- Keep your shoulders and hips level at all times.
- When you hit your last step on all the drops—three, five, and seven—make sure that your back foot is underneath your hips and shoulders so that your weight is always centered.
- Don't overextend your last step and lean forward at the same time to break your momentum, or you may slip and fall.
- Use the five-step drop for throwing long and the seven for maneuver routes.
- When you begin to learn any of these drops, start at a very slow pace. Once you get the rhythm down, you'll be able to increase your speed to the level needed in competition.

STRONG FUNDAMENTALS: Ever since I was a kid, I was taught to stand tall in the pocket and to hold the ball high. My dad taught me the fundamentals in our backyard while I practiced for the Punt, Pass, and Kick competitions. In junior high, my brother Ray taught me that I must hold the ball high so that I would get a quick and high release. This would prevent the ball being knocked down at the line of scrimmage. And Terry Bradshaw showed me how to grip the ball so that I would throw a tight spiral.

—Jim Kelly

Quarterback, Buffalo Bills

Figure 3.22a

Figure 3.22b

Figure 3.22c

Look at my back leg and foot as I've landed. My knee is slightly bent. My weight is in the ball of my foot with my heel up and rotated slightly outward. A quick pivot the rest of the way outward makes it easier and more efficient to step to my left and open my hips to throw.

the basics

Figure 3.23 What's wrong with this picture? I'm moving toward the line of scrimmage but I've already squared my shoulders to the line. If my shoulders were in the right position, you should be able to read the number eleven on my chest. My options are limited now. I can't rotate my hips or do anything with my body to generate power behind the ball. The pass had better be something fairly short.

POCKET DRILL

The **pocket drill** is one of the best ways I know to reinforce the basic techniques of moving with the ball in the pocket. Now that we've covered the three-, five-, and seven-step drops, you've got enough technique under your belt to use this drill effectively. Remember to keep your movement as efficient as possible. The whole idea of the pocket drill is moving in the pocket to avoid tacklers and to stay in the position to throw the football. To do that effectively, you must keep your hips and shoulders perpendicular to the line of scrimmage or parallel to the sideline. The worst thing you can do is to turn your hips and shoulders parallel to the line of scrimmage and run toward it to throw. Once you do that, as a right-handed passer, you make it nearly impossible to throw the ball to the right (Figure 3.23). The pocket drill will also help you to learn how to move efficiently in the pocket, a step at a time: forward and backward, left and right. You won't need a center for this drill. Begin by standing in position to receive the ball as if there were a center in front of you. Your coach should be standing in front of you, on the defensive side of the ball. Hold the ball as if it had just been snapped to you: head up, chin out, looking downfield. Make sure that your shoulders are square, your weight is over your hips, and your knees are slightly bent. Use bottom-hand pressure as you stand pigeon-toed, under center. Your coach will be about five yards away. Start by taking a five-step drop, remembering to protect the ball as you move. Carry it with two hands, chest high, elbows in, and your shoulders relaxed. Keep the ball close to your body and under control with front-hand pressure. You should be ready to throw the football. Now look at your feet when you land. They should be shoulder width apart, with your toes pointed at the sideline. Your front foot

the basics

Figure 3.24

Figure 3.25

Figure 3.26

Figure 3.27

should be slightly in front of your back foot: A line drawn from the toe of your back foot toward the line of scrimmage would pass through the instep of your front foot (Figure 3.24).

Remember to keep your left shoulder in good throwing position: perpendicular to the line of scrimmage and pointing downfield as you watch the coach to see his hand signals. If the coach points toward the sideline in front of you, push off your front foot, and step *forward* with your back foot. Then recover your front foot again so you're in good throwing position, with your front foot slightly in front of the back, toes toward the sideline. The rhythm is **push—one, two** and you're in position to throw (Figure 3.25). The **one-two** is more of a shuffle than anything else: two quick steps with your feet barely off the ground. Say it to yourself as you begin. Push off your front foot, step with your back foot, then step with your front foot: **push—one, two**. If the coach points to the sideline behind you, take one step back, pushing off of your front foot (Figure 3.26). This is your leverage foot. Push off your front foot, and step with your back foot. Then recover your front foot again to the throwing position: just slightly ahead of the other, toes still pointing to the sideline. Again, the rhythm is **push—one, two**. Say it to yourself as you do it: **push—one, two**.

Movement toward the line of scrimmage works a little differently. When the coach points toward the line, push off your back foot and glide one step toward the line with your front foot. Then recover the back foot by sliding it into position again, under the hips and shoulders. The motion is **push and glide** (Figure 3.27). Say that to yourself as you begin. Push off the back foot and glide on the front foot. **Push and glide**. Once again, you should finish in good throw-

the basics

SEEING THE RESULTS: I was really surprised as I began to notice the effects of what Jim Fassel was teaching us in drills like the pocket drill or the slap drill. We worked on them every day in practice and wondered sometimes what difference they made. But as the season progressed, we all began to see the results. There were games during which I didn't consciously realize I had done something, but the next day, when the coaches showed me the film, I'd be standing there in the pocket, waiting, looking down the field as a defender took a slap at the ball. And I'd just move it, just a little. I did it, but I don't remember consciously making the decision to shift the ball out of the way. I guess it was becoming instinctive by then. And I just laughed when I saw it and thought it was pretty cool. It was a little thing, just a slight move of the hands while I focused on my receivers, but it gave me a second more in the pocket. And one more second is one more chance to make a positive play and avoid getting sacked or stripped of the ball. That second wasn't the difference in that game, but I knew it would be sometime soon.

—P.S.

ing position, feet shoulder width apart. Remember to keep your knees slightly bent, with your hips and shoulders level.

A big mistake many quarterbacks make as they move toward the line is to rise up. They stand up taller to see the rush better. I've seen them get right up on the balls of their feet. And once you stand straight up like that, you're not in the position anymore to push off your back foot and rotate your hips as you're throwing the football. The other common error you'll see is the tendency for players to hop toward the line of scrimmage as they move forward in the pocket. The body is up, the shoulders are tilted up in front, and the passer is pushing off the back foot in a hopping motion. Quarterbacks who hop like this have difficulty throwing the ball quickly with any power.

They're off balance and they have no leverage on the ball. Any throw from this position is all arm. With the shoulders tilted upward like this, the tendency is to get too much weight loaded up on your back foot so you can't transfer forward again quickly enough. The tendency in this position is to throw the ball high. Think about it. It makes sense. If the shoulders are pointed up, the ball's going to go up.

As you've done with every other drill we've covered, start off slowly and master the steps first. Work in slow motion, a step at a time, and build up your speed gradually. This one of those times where effective, fluid motion is very important. Rushing to gain speed before you master technique just magnifies bad habits.

A typical series of moves would start off with a whistle to begin your five-step drop. Your coach would then give you about three or four directions, pointing in the direction he wants you to go, one step at a time. Again, this is not a speed drill. We're simulating one-step moves here to avoid pressure from an advancing defenseman or to move into a better position to throw the ball. Take your time and do it right so that it becomes your natural motion under game conditions.

the basics

Figure 3.28a   **Figure 3.28b**

Slap Drill

The **slap drill** (Figure 3.28) is a two-man exercise and it's very simple. The quarterback does a three-, five-, or seven-step drop and the other person slaps at the ball once as he moves and sets to throw. Vary the time of the slap and the direction of it. One time you might hit down on the ball. Another time you might hit from underneath or the side. The object is to make sure you're carrying the ball with two hands, with front-hand pressure to protect it. This drill will help you to build confidence in moving with the ball under pressure.

CHAPTER 4

The Grip

Figure 4.0   Kansas City, 1984. Look at the right foot. The heel is off the ground, as it should be. My weight is concentrated on the inside edge of the ball of my right foot and my right knee as I get ready to stride into a pass. I have the leverage I need to push off and throw with power. The ball is a little low but acceptable. My shoulders and arms are loose and the grip is relaxed.

Remember, consistently good passing mechanics begin with the little things you do correctly over and over again. For instance, the way you place your fingers on the football when you throw can make a huge difference in your performance. It can affect your accuracy, your velocity, and even the physical condition of your throwing arm. I used to experiment a lot with different grips, and I kept track of all the different ways quarterbacks around the league held the ball when they threw. What I found is that the vast majority fell into two categories: the **one-and-fours** and the **two-and-fives**.

Figure 4.1a

Figure 4.1b

Figure 4.2

Figure 4.3

John Elway, for example, is a one-and-four gripper. That is, he holds the ball so that his ring finger covers the first lace and his little finger covers the fourth (Figure 4.1). Dan Marino holds the ball so that his fingers cover the second and fifth laces (Figure 4.2). I'm also a two-and-fiver, but I started off with a variation of the two-and-five. I remember when I was in fifth grade, looking down at my hand as I held the ball and saying to myself, "Second and fifth." Only then, my little finger was under the fifth lace (Figure 4.3).

Eventually, as I threw the ball harder, I had to modify my grip a little because it made my elbow sore. I discovered that holding the football with my little finger under the lace made me squeeze the ball harder to hold on to it. I'll talk about why that can be harmful, but first let me say that when I adjusted my grip so that my little finger went over the lace, the pain went away. I found that I had better control and I could secure the ball without so much finger pressure.

Figure 4.4

That's really the key: holding the football in a way that feels comfortable to you with the least amount of strain. Every quarterback has his own particular way of throwing the ball. Troy Aikman of the Dallas Cowboys, for example, holds the ball so that the laces cross the palm of his hand (Figure 4.4). It works for him, but it's not something I would do.

I can't look at you and say, "You're a two-and-fiver." You really have to pick up the football, move it around in your hand, and experiment a little to see what works best for your particular throwing motion.

LIGHT GRIP/LOOSE ARM

One of the first things that Jim Fassel stresses is keeping a light grip on the football as you throw. Overgripping (gripping the ball too hard) tends to tighten up the muscles in the forearm and the shoulder. It consumes arm strength and keeps you from getting a full range of motion when you throw. To avoid injury and soreness, it is crucial to keep your arm loose throughout the throwing motion.

the grip

Figure 4.5   Looks good, but what's wrong here? I'm overstriding. My step is so long that no matter what I do, I'm going to have trouble shifting my weight over to the left foot to complete the throwing sequence with power. So I'll probably slide under the ball because it's the only way I can finish the throw.

Overgripping is the most frequent mistake I see among quarterbacks at all levels, including the pros. As I said, it was a problem I had on and off for years. Before I worked with Jim, I tried a lot of different grips. At times, I was squeezing the ball pretty hard. I found that the harder I'd squeeze, the less control I'd have. I'd lose flexibility in my arm and then find myself trying to muscle the ball to the target (Figure 4.5). And that opens up a whole world of other potential problems that I'll get into later.

Nature has a way of getting your attention when you're doing something wrong, and it's usually painful. There were days when I'd finish practice and my arm would really ache, deep in my shoulder and my elbow. It got that way from throwing with tight muscles, caused by gripping the ball too hard. That's probably the best early-warning sign you'll ever find. Long before a coach may notice, your own body will tell you, loud and clear. Once I started gripping the ball lightly, I could throw all day and never get a sore arm.

When you grip the ball, there should only be the slightest bit of tension in your arm. Anything more than that and you're doing it wrong. The ball has got to be held in such a way that you don't feel tightness in your forearm or shoulder. When you throw the football, your arm should move like a whip. And it can't move that way when the muscles are tense. The arm has to be loose to work efficiently in the throwing motion.

ON THE FINGERTIPS
We talk about gripping the ball with your hand but we actually mean the tips of your fingers. The ball should *not* rest in the

SQUEEZING TOO HARD: I always looked for different grips. And now, when I look back on it, there's no question in my mind why I was looking for them. It was because I was squeezing the ball so tightly. I was looking for an easier way to squeeze it. The odd thing is that the harder I squeezed, the less I felt like I had a good grip. I didn't grip the ball lightly until my last few years. So for most of my career, I guess you could say I was a squeezer. I liked to throw the older footballs, too. They were great for me because they were softer and not slick, as the new ones can be. I could squeeze those things to death. And I would, too. That's why, as I look back now, I had trouble with some balls. I was definitely squeezing too hard.

But every rule has its exception. I've talked to a lot of pros about the way they grip the ball. One of them is one of the game's top quarterbacks today and an

Figure 4.6a

Figure 4.6b

Grip the ball with the pads of your fingers. You should be able to slide a pencil between the ball and the palm of your hand (Figure 4.6b).

palm of your hand at all (Figure 4.6). In fact, you should be able to slide a pencil between the palm of your hand and the ball as you hold it to throw.

excellent passer. He told me that he squeezes the ball as hard as he can. And he says some days, when he comes off the practice field, his forearm hurts so bad he can't even think. It feels like it's going to explode. I was surprised, but apparently he's done it this way for so long that by the time the next day comes around, his arm feels good. He can go out there and squeeze it again.

He says that the only time squeezing becomes a problem for him is when the ball gets wet. The conventional wisdom was that if the ball got wet, you tried to grip it tighter. Today, given what I've learned, I would say you shouldn't tighten the grip for a wet ball. If anything, you should loosen it a little. Loosen it for more control, and maybe slow down the whole sequence of throwing a little. Try to perfect the mechanics of your throwing motion.

—P.S.

the grip

It's like shooting a basketball. You don't rest the ball on your palm. All the sensitivity, dexterity, and control you need come from the pads of your fingers as you follow through to the basket. That same principle applies in throwing the football.

Now this may sound like a contradiction, but in order to hold the ball as loosely as you should, you need to build up the strength in your fingers. The theory is that if the muscles in your hand and forearm are sufficiently developed, you will only need a fraction of your total strength to hold the ball, leaving the rest of the muscles loose and flexible.

Look at it this way. Let's say you're capable of holding a hundred pounds in your hand, and I'm telling you to hold the ball with 10 percent of your potential grip pressure. That's ten pounds. Now if you were able to double the strength in your arm so you could hold two hundred pounds in that hand, 10 percent would be twenty pounds. You would still apply only 10 percent of your total strength to holding the football, but now, because you're stronger, that 10 percent equals twenty pounds of grip pressure. The result is a sure grip with a relaxed feeling.

There is no shortage of exercises and equipment out there to help you build up hand strength—balls and spring grippers and such— but one of the most effective is also the simplest and the least expensive. All it takes is a newspaper (Figure 4.7).

Pull out a full page, open it, and lay it flat on your kitchen table or the floor of the family room. Now place your throwing hand flat down in the center of the page and begin to gather up the paper, using your fingers. Keep on wadding up the paper with your fingers until it's a tight ball in the palm of your hand. Hold the wad of paper for about five or six seconds and then release it. Repeat the exercise a few times at first and gradually build up the number of pages as your strength grows.

Figure 4.7a

Figure 4.7b

Figure 4.8a

Figure 4.8b

Some people like to squeeze a tennis ball. Others use spring grippers or exercise putty. I also recommend building up your wrists and hands using a device that has a small weight connected to one end of a four-foot length of rope with other end attached to the center of a stick or bar of some kind (Figure 4.8).

Hold on to the bar at both ends, extending your arms out in front of you, chest high with bar parallel to the floor, and roll up the rope on the bar until the weight is chest high off the floor. Then reverse the motion so that you lower the weight back to the floor under control. The exercise is effective in both directions, so take it slow.

I also like to do a couple of drills that are very simple and don't require anything more than the object with which you're trying to get familiar and proficient—the football.

Figure 4.9

In the first exercise (Figure 4.9), you get down on one knee (left knee for a right-handed thrower) and drop the ball from your throwing hand and catch it before it bounces. The idea is to catch it with the same hand. It will take some practice before you can do it consistently but it's a great drill for building up your finger strength and your reflexes.

the grip

Figure 4.10

The second ball drill involves a buddy (Figure 4.10). In this one you hold the ball in your throwing hand straight out in front of you. Have your buddy grab the ball from the other side and pull until someone loses his grip. Do four or five repetitions, go on to something else, and then come back and do a few more.

Don't try to do all of these exercises every day. Pick a few and then mix and match them two or three times a week so your workouts don't get boring. Remember, the whole idea here is to build up strength in the throwing hand so that you are using only a fraction of your total strength to grip the football. Ideally, it should just about fall out of your hand when you hold it palm down.

CHAPTER 5
Throwing the Football

Figure 5.0   1984 playoff game. I'm really turning and coming forward. Look at the angle of the back leg. I've already pushed off. My weight is already on my front foot and I'm driving my left elbow down. When I threw this ball, I had tremendous rotation on it with my hips and shoulders coming forward. (I'm in a crowd but I'm totally focused. Through practice you just forget that they're there.)

PHIL WHO?

During the 1978–1979 season, Morehead State had not done particularly well, and the knock on Phil Simms at the time among the scouts was that he wasn't a winner. This was the scout mentality, anyhow. You have to understand that. It was a very simplistic evaluation. Morehead had four wins and five losses—something like that. The scouts' attitude was that this guy couldn't be a great prospect if Morehead didn't win with him.

GETTING THERE: Sam Wyche and I needed a quarterback that year, and we visited just about every college quarterback in the country. So, we went down to Morehead State. Getting there was unbelievable. This place was so out of the way that I had to charter a plane. We left out of Cincinnati, and it was the most harrowing flight I've ever had in my life. The weather got bad and the pilot couldn't see. When we finally found the place, the runway was eight hundred feet shorter than the map said. We looked around and there wasn't one other aircraft at the airport. The terminal was an old mobile home with a wind sock hanging on a pole outside. It looked like something out of a Hollywood movie set. So we circled that thing and circled it and finally the pilot said he'd give it a try, and we landed, stopping about fifty feet from the end of the runway. Now this place wasn't out in the open like some place in Nebraska. There were tall pine trees all around us. So you had to be a bush pilot to get in there. Once we were on the ground, there was no way to get to town. We found out that nobody ever goes to that airport. It took nearly an hour to get a cab. There were only two cabs in town, and the one that came for us got lost trying to find the airport.

We finally met Phil, and he was a great guy. We watched films together and then we went out on the field and worked out. Later, we went and had a couple of big meals. And when I left, I felt that Phil would be the guy that we would draft. The trip had been worth it. I hadn't seen Joe Montana yet, but in my mind Phil was the guy. And I honestly thought we could get Phil because of the scouting reports and the out-of-the-way location and all. I thought we could get Phil in the third round. That was our pick. I really felt that we might have a chance. So I was excited when I told Sam, this is the guy. He had a really strong arm. He was a terrific athlete and he had a great football mentality—everything I wanted. Well, by the time the draft came along, the shrewd people in the league had figured it out and the Giants drafted him in the first round.

—Bill Walsh

Retired Head Coach, Stanford University
Former Head Coach, San Francisco 49ers

throwing the football

Almost every pro coach who put me through a workout when I was finishing my senior year at Morehead State said the same thing: "Throw it as hard as you can." They wanted to see how far I could throw the football. I always asked them what they'd like me to do, thinking it might be different. But it was about the same every time.

THE WORKOUT:

I had come to the realization after working with so many quarterbacks and having so much exposure to the game that every pass play is a different kind of throw. At times you really want to drill the ball. But most of the time it's an arching throw over a linebacker's head or between people. What you want is a soft throw with a tight spiral. And Phil had not done that at all. He was really a strong, quick-armed guy who didn't have much of a touch. In college, they never worked on it. So I put him through a lot of drills where we pretended that he had to throw over this guy or around that guy. And then I told him you can drill this pass...and when you throw it deep, you throw it this way. I said that every pass play takes a different kind of throw. A third baseman throwing to first base is different from a second baseman throwing to first. It's different from an outfielder throwing into the infield. They're all different throws. In football, every kind of throw has to be practiced, and at that time Phil had never really done that. And to this day, very few people do.

—Bill Walsh
Retired Head Coach, Stanford University
Former Head Coach, San Francisco 49ers

Bill Walsh was the exception. He's retired now, but at the time, he was getting ready to start his first year as the head coach of the San Francisco 49ers. I didn't know it then, but he was and probably still is one of the most knowledgeable quarterback coaches around.

That afternoon, when Coach Walsh met me down at the field, I asked him the usual question, expecting the normal drill. But instead, he looked at me and in this soft voice he has, almost whispering, he said, "I want you to drop back, Phil. Just glide, and when you hit that back foot, throw the ball as pretty as you can throw it. Make it a perfect spiral every time. It should just float in the air and drop into the receiver's hands." It sounded like poetry...and about the easiest workout I would ever have.

So, we started. I'd throw the ball and he'd say, "That's great. That's perfect. Throw it a little softer now." And before I knew it, I was throwing the ball as far as, maybe even farther than, I had thrown it in my other workouts, when I was trying to throw it hard. But these passes were dead-on accurate and catchable.

That was 1979. The Giants drafted me ahead of the 49ers. Ray Perkins became my coach. And I never really gave Bill Walsh or what he was saying much thought again, at least not for a long time. As I said, his philosophy was not the norm in those days. The accepted practice was to throw hard. And I remember passing in my early years as a pro. Balls would be right there, in their hands, and receivers would drop them. I'd be drilling them right in the numbers and I couldn't understand why they didn't hold on. And the coaches would say "It's not your fault." Well, I know now that, in fact, many times, it *was* my fault. I was just throwing the ball too hard.

Bottom line: The only thing that matters is whether or not the receiver catches the ball. Regardless of the situation, regardless of the weather or field conditions, first and foremost, the ball has got to be catchable. That's the quarterback's job. It wasn't until I

throwing the football

started working with Jim Fassel that I learned the techniques I needed to throw a consistently more accurate and catchable pass, a goal *his* mentor, Bill Walsh, had tried to teach me fourteen years earlier. I just didn't understand.

THE WHOLE BODY

The most important concept to remember about throwing the football is that it's a full-body motion. Solid throwing fundamentals begin in the feet and legs and continue through the hips, shoulders, and elbow, right down to the fingertips. Lose or weaken any element in that chain and you drain power and create problems, some of which can cause injury.

One word of caution before we get into specific elements of throwing: As you study and practice these techniques, begin slowly, at half-speed, and master the form in detail. One of the biggest mistakes I see in coaches and players alike is that they rush the process of learning. Walk through the drills as you start. Take your time. Speed and distance will come with practice and time.

A THROWING PHILOSOPHY

One of the first things I ask aspiring quarterbacks is to tell me how far they think they could pass the ball standing flat-footed on the line of scrimmage, without moving their feet. After a few estimates and tries we usually come to the conclusion that it's not very far.

The best you might get is thirty yards or so—and that's if you have a great arm. Then I tell them to get back ten yards, five yards...one yard, if they want to, before they throw the football. The distance doesn't matter: just so you can move toward the line of scrimmage as you throw the ball. I ask them which way they think you can throw the ball farther. And, of course, they agree that the ball will go farther when you're moving, when you're propelling yourself toward the line of scrimmage and the target as you throw.

That's really the basic philosophy of throwing the football effectively: Regardless of your position, you want to create momentum toward your target, to get your body behind the ball and move it toward the receiver as you pass. I'm not talking about running toward the line and launching the ball. I'm talking about the contained movement of your body within a stride as you throw (see Chapter 7, Figure 7.5). When that movement is executed, it will harness all the energy you can generate in your legs, hips, and shoulders and transfer it into the ball as it's released. That's what this approach to passing is all about. Every drill and exercise is intended to teach you how to get your body into position so you can transfer its power to the football. If you learn these mechanics and understand what you're trying to do and why, you'll become a better passer. You'll be able to throw the football farther and with greater accuracy.

THROWING THE FOOTBALL

For the sake of simplicity, we'll begin throwing to a receiver ten yards down the center of the field, from a straight three-step drop. What I'm going to do is generally describe the full motion of throwing and then go back and look at the finer details. Keep in mind that the whole purpose of these mechanics is to get your body behind the ball, moving toward the line of scrimmage and your target when you throw.

throwing the football

Figure 5.1a   Figure 5.1b   Figure 5.1c

Figure 5.1d   Figure 5.1e   Figure 5.1f

Begin by standing in the middle of the field, about ten yards away from your receiver, with your toes pointing toward the sideline (Figure 5.1). Your feet should be parallel and shoulder width apart, with your left foot slightly ahead of your right. A line drawn from the toe of your right foot would intersect your left foot at the instep. As you stand there, your weight should be concentrated more on the inside of your right foot and knee. In this position, you should be looking over your left shoulder (for a right-handed passer) which is pointed down the field at your receiver. Hold the ball in both hands, relaxed and a few inches away from your body at about midchest. Remember, your elbows should be down...and your shoulders level and loose. Both your knees should be slightly bent so your hips drop slightly. How much?

Well, I'm about six two standing with my knees straight. When I'm standing in the pocket preparing to throw, I'm about six one. It's not much of a bend but it makes all the difference in the world to your balance and mobility as you move and throw the football.

When you step forward with your left foot to throw, push off your right foot to propel your body forward with the step. Make it a comfortable stride. Don't lunge or get too spread out. Land on your left foot, heel first, and finish the step so that your knee remains slightly bent. Your foot should land, toes pointing downfield, ahead of your intended receiver. As you step and push off, you'll feel your weight shifting out of your right foot and into your left. At the same time push the ball back toward your right shoulder with front-hand pressure until you naturally release it into your throwing hand to cock the ball into throwing position. This motion will leave your left (non-throwing) arm high across your chest. As soon as you release the ball with that left hand, drive your left elbow down and back so that you pull your shoulders, hips, and throwing arm forward, toward your target. Your throwing arm will lag slightly behind your shoulders as it whips forward to catch up to the rest of your body.

Remember what you're trying to create here: momentum going forward toward your target, arm lagging behind so you can whip it forward to put speed on the ball. If your throwing arm is loose when you release the ball, your throwing hand will rotate naturally across your body to the opposite hip. Your palm will finish down, with your fingers pointing at the ground. Follow through so that your weight ends up entirely on your front foot as you complete your long and relaxed follow-through. Some coaches say you should be able to pull a dollar bill out of your left pocket as you finish.

throwing the football

The complete motion works like a slingshot or a catapult. Shifting your weight to your right foot and pushing the ball back into throwing position is like stretching the rubber band or pulling down the catapult arm. Stepping forward and driving the left arm down and back releases the mechanism and delivers a burst of energy to the ball through your arm as it whips forward to catch up.

| Figure 5.2a | Figure 5.2b | Figure 5.2c |

| Figure 5.2d | Figure 5.2e |

A CLOSER LOOK

Shifting your weight onto your back foot is a natural result of any drop as you land on the last step. They key to doing it effectively is landing so that your weight is concentrated on the inside portion of the ball of your right foot and knee. Your heel should be slightly off the ground. In this position you are ready to push off immediately as you step forward to throw the football (Figure 5.2). If you land flat-footed and push off, you won't generate the immediate power that you get when you push off the ball of your foot. And if you land flat-footed and then reposition your foot, you're adding wasted motion.

Try it. Do a three-step drop and land on your back foot so that it lands flat, with your heel on the ground. Push off and throw the ball. It probably feels okay. Now land so that your weight is in the ball of your foot and your heel is slightly off the ground. You really can feel the difference. The response is much more immediate and powerful. As you step to throw, the weight shift to your front foot will happen almost automatically if you push off your back foot and really drive your left elbow down and back. It's this combination of actions that generates and transfers power to your throwing arm. You can't consistently generate that kind of power with your arm alone without eventually causing damage.

Watch John Elway as he throws the ball the next time a Denver game is televised. Notice how his head turns as he drives his nonpassing elbow down and back, leaving his passing arm behind momentarily. The power in his passing motion is not coming so much from his arm strength as it is from his legs and the action of his shoulders and hips. It's a very powerful motion. John throws the ball hard, but if you look closely, you'll see that his throwing arm and hand are loose and relaxed as he whips them forward and releases the ball.

5–4–3–1–2

Anatomically, the fingers are numbered 1 through 5, starting with the thumb and ending with the little finger. When you throw the football, your fingers come off the ball in reverse order, with the exception of the thumb and middle finger (Figure 5.3). They come off together. So the order is 5–4–3–1–2. Stated another way, when your throwing hand gets to the top of the throwing motion and it naturally starts to rotate forward and down, the little finger should come off the ball first, then your ring finger,

throwing the football

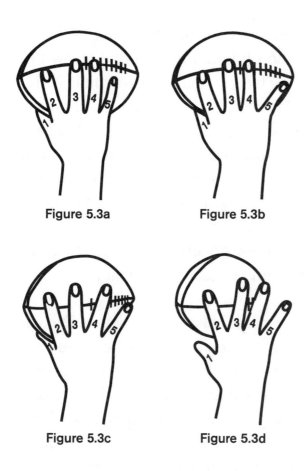

Figure 5.3a   Figure 5.3b

Figure 5.3c   Figure 5.3d

followed by your middle finger and thumb. Last off is your index finger. Jim Fassel calls this last finger off the ball the **guide finger**. Others call it the **pusher finger**. In either case, it provides the last push on the ball and determines its attitude in flight. Properly thrown, the ball will fly with the nose slightly upward and to the right (for a right-handed passer) because of the pressure you're exerting on the tail of the ball as you release it. The pressure should be downward and in as your hand completes its motion across your body. Quarterbacks who throw the ball enough will actually get a small callus on the inside edge of the tip of the index finger. It's caused by the friction of the ball against the last point of contact.

FORM DRILL

One of the best ways I know to help you learn to relax and follow through is to work with a partner, throwing the ball to each other in a complete, exaggerated motion. Begin by standing about ten yards apart so you can pass the ball to each other. Don't just toss it back and forth. Each time you throw, I want you to step, throw, and follow through with perfect form, shoulders and hips level

Figure 5.4a

Figure 5.4b

Figure 5.4c

Figure 5.4d

Figure 5.4e

Figure 5.4f

(Figure 5.4). See if you can deliver the ball as softly as you can, on target every time. Start slowly. Step and push off your back foot. Land heel-toe and bend your knee slightly. Drive your non-passing arm down and back so that you pull your shoulders and hips forward, toward your target. Keep your throwing arm loose so it whips through your delivery. Grip the ball comfortably, and keep your wrist loose so your hand turns over naturally and follows through to your opposite hip. When you do it this way, you can feel the mechanics working. You can feel the transfer of power from your legs through your hips and shoulders to your arm. You can feel your arm lag slightly behind and whip forward to catch up.

throwing the football

In this drill you should concentrate solely on technique. You're not trying to throw the ball for distance or speed. You're completing every detail of the passing motion, slowly and deliberately, for the sole purpose of building the habits of good fundamental form. I used to do this drill on the sideline as part of my warm-up before every game. It not only helped me get my arm and body loose, but it also reinforced the good mechanics I'd need for the day. Remember, the first thing that suffers when you try to create force on the ball is technique. The harder you try to throw, the more you will magnify any deficiencies you have in your fundamental form. As the old saying goes, you've got to learn how to walk before you can run, or you'll fall flat on your face.

If you try to throw the ball with velocity before you've perfected the full chain of events in the throwing motion, you'll likely develop bad habits that will cost you somewhere down the road. A drill like the one I've just described will help you to develop solid technique so that when you need both accuracy and velocity, you don't have to create one at expense of the other.

PASSING CHECKLIST
- Toes facing sidelines
- Front shoulder pointed downfield
- Feet shoulder width apart
- Front foot slightly ahead of back foot
- Weight concentrated on ball of back foot (inside portion) and knee
- Ball in both hands, chest high
- Shoulders relaxed, elbows down
- Shoulders and hips level
- Knees slightly bent

throwing the football

TOUCH

A quarterback has to have touch with the football. He's got to know when to fire it in there and when not to. Distance is the biggest factor. As a tight end or a running back, you don't want the quarterback to be smoking the football to you on a ten-yard pattern. That's a problem for a lot of quarterbacks. They don't know when to take the heat off of the ball. On short patterns, you're usually talking about split seconds. You turn your head and a lot of times the ball is in the air. It's coming at you and you've got to react instantaneously. And when a ball's coming in with heat, you won't have time to prepare yourself for it. It's going to go right through your hands. In the worst-case scenario, it will go right through your hands and bounce off your helmet right into the hands of a defender for an interception.

—Mark Bavaro
Tight End, New York Giants
1985–1990

- Step with front foot and push off back foot
- Push ball to back shoulder and release into passing hand
- Drive nonpassing elbow down and back
- Throwing arm relaxed
- Movement of shoulders and hips toward target initiates throwing motion
- Throwing hand follows through after release to opposite hip

Figure 5.5a

Figure 5.5b

THE BALL NEVER LIES

Jim Fassel told me many times that he really didn't need to see me throw the ball to tell me what I was doing wrong. All he had to do was watch the flight of the ball on its way to the receiver. He used to say that the ball never lies. When I'd throw one into the ground on a twenty-yard route up the middle, he knew that I had probably locked out my left knee as I stepped to throw. We'd look at the game film and he'd usually be right. Most quarterbacks will do that when they land toe-first as they step forward to throw. Try it and you'll see that your knee just straightens out (Figure 5.5). This stops your hips from rotating and keeps your body from moving forward. Once your knee is locked out, the only way to generate the power you need is to throw your upper body forward, over your front leg. When you do that, the ball goes down because that's where the force generated by the body is directed.

The other element to consider here is the motion of your arm. When you throw properly, with the knees slightly bent, your throwing arm will complete its full range of motion to deliver the ball. It travels from the cocked position in a full arc to finish at the opposite hip. But if you lock the knee and your body doesn't rotate forward as it should, what happens? The arm motion has to be shorter. Your range of motion is limited by your body position. When you throw your body forward over your locked knee to get power, the shortened arm motion magnifies the error and the ball travels downward most of the time. Try it. You can feel the difference when you throw your body over the locked knee. The throwing motion feels rushed and out of rhythm compared to a bent knee delivery. You cannot follow through.

So if you're throwing a lot of balls into the dirt, it's probably because you're not landing your front foot heel-toe. You're landing toe-heel and locking out your front leg.

Figure 5.6a

Figure 5.6b

Now, what if you're having the opposite problem and throwing the ball high? Think about it. Ideally, you want your hips and shoulders level when you pass the ball. When you're throwing the ball high, it's usually because you're letting your hips get out in front of the rest of your body as you step to throw. When you do that, your throwing shoulder naturally drops and your front shoulder pitches up. Look at the position of your body (Figure 5.6).

You may be looking straight and level, but your upper body is pointing up. Your hips are already forward so you can't generate any power there. It's all got to come from your upper body, from your arm. Most quarterbacks in this position will drop their throwing elbow to try to compensate for the pitch of their shoulders, but the ball will usually rise anyhow because that's where the body is facing; that's where the shoulders are pointed.

throwing the football

| Figure 5.7a | Figure 5.7b | Figure 5.7c |

| Figure 5.7d | Figure 5.7e | Figure 5.7f |

THROWING LONG

Every rule seems to have its exception. And when it comes to throwing the football, the exception comes into play when we talk about throwing the ball longer distances (more than forty yards). Remember, we said that you want to keep your body centered, your shoulders and hips level, and your knees slightly bent as you throw the ball (Figure 5.7). You should even drop your front shoulder a bit to make sure your delivery is mechanically sound. When you throw long, a lot of things change.

The key to throwing long successfully is releasing the ball with a more upward trajectory, with the nose of the ball more to the sky (Figure 5.8). You want to look that way and throw that way. Instead

Figure 5.8a

Figure 5.8b

Figure 5.8c

Figure 5.8d

Figure 5.8e

Figure 5.8f

Figure 5.8g

Explode off the back foot to propel your upper body over your front leg (5.8f). I've exaggerated the follow-through so you can really see the weight transfer.

throwing the football

of looking directly at your receiver, you want to pick out a spot in the air above him. What happens when you look up? Try it. Get into your normal stance to throw the ball and then look up. You can feel more weight shift onto your back foot for balance. Your

Figure 5.9a   Figure 5.9b   Figure 5.9c

Figure 5.9d   Figure 5.9e   Figure 5.9f

Figure 5.9g

front shoulder comes up, and your back shoulder drops. Now as you step and throw from this position, the difficulty comes in getting your weight over to your front foot as you release the ball. Because of the steeper angle of your shoulders, you really have to

Figure 5.10a

Figure 5.10b

Figure 5.10c

Figure 5.10d

throw your upper body over your front leg. You have to explode off the back foot and make a conscious effort to propel your upper body forward.

WHAT CAN GO WRONG

Many quarterbacks make the mistake of staying on their back leg too long so that they let their hips slide way out in front of them. They let their throwing shoulder drop too far down as their hips pitch up in front. Thrown this way, the ball goes up and dies (Figure 5.9). That's because the passer is releasing the ball before he can shift his weight from his back leg to the front. So the ball just floats and falls short. You can't generate enough momentum with your arms alone. You want to explode off the back foot and get your body over to the front leg quickly, so that all that power is transferred to the ball as you release it (Figure 5.10). Thrown properly, the ball will fly with an upward trajectory and then nose over to the receiver (Figure 5.11). If it doesn't nose over, you didn't get your upper body over the top in time. It's as simple as that. Remember, the ball never lies.

throwing the football

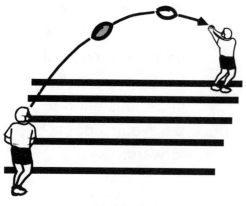

Figure 5.11

One last point. Practice your long passes with a five-step drop. Remember, most of your long routes will be run from a five. A seven is too long. By the time you're ready to throw a post or a seam route from a seven-step drop, you'd be trying to put the ball out there eighty yards or so. I'd be hard pressed to reach my slowest receiver from a seven-step drop. The only time you'd use a seven-step drop on a long route is if your receiver is running a double pattern; then you might need the extra time.

RHYTHM PAT

The next time you watch a pro game on TV, make it a point to watch the motion of the quarterback's hand and the ball just before he throws. Watch closely and you'll see that just before he pushes the ball back into its cocked position to throw, he will take his front hand off the ball for an instant, tap the ball against the palm of his front hand again, and then cock and throw it. This called a **rhythm pat**. And there is a rhythm to it. A lot of coaches teach it. It starts the throwing motion, and it releases whatever tension there is in your body.

When you drop to throw, you carry the ball chest high with both hands. As you land, front-hand pressure pushes the ball closer to the throwing position. There's a rhythm to your motion in the pocket as you retreat from the line. There's a rhythm to the way you land and gather yourself to throw. The rhythm pat inserts that

PLACEMENT

Most receivers want the ball right in the stomach-to-chest area because even in traffic you can catch it and cover up. Very rarely do you want the ball over your head. When you get to the higher levels of the game, most receivers want to be able to keep their arms down so they can protect their ribs. That's why you see a lot of guys short-arm the ball. If the ball goes over their head, they don't reach out for it. There are all sorts of nicknames for it: Alligator Arms, Dino (the pet from *The Flintstones*), Venus de Milo, and so on.

—Mark Bavaro
Tight End, New York Giants
1985–1990

same body rhythm into the passing motion. You drop, land, pat, and throw. It's a natural thing to do. It releases tension and gets your upper body loose and ready to throw. So I would never discourage you from taking a rhythm pat.

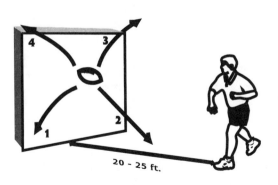

20 - 25 ft.

Figure 5.12

THROWING AGAINST THE WALL

Jim Fassel has a great test that you or your coach can use to see if you're throwing the ball correctly, with the most effective attitude and spin (Figure 5.12). Grab a ball and stand

Figure 5.13a

Figure 5.13b

Figure 5.13c

Figure 5.13d

Figure 5.13e

A three-step drop should put you in position to throw the football as you land on the third step. Your receivers will be running short, timing patterns, so the rhythm of the drop and pass combined should feel like one, two, push, land, and throw. There's really no time to do anything else. Don't rush. Keep the rhythm. Take your first step away from center so that your hips open up all the way and your foot lands directly away from the line of scrimmage. Carry the ball with two hands, chest high, elbows in and loose. Your front shoulder should be pointed downfield, and your chest facing the sideline. As you take your second step, the crossover step, turn from looking straight downfield to find your primary receiver and start to push the football back into throwing position with front-hand pressure. As you land, your back heel should be slightly of the ground

Figure 5.13f

Figure 5.13g

and your weight concentrated on the inside portion of the ball of your back foot and knee. As you step forward to throw, land heel to toe so that your front foot is pointed to where your receiver will be when he should catch the ball. Push off your back foot, drive your nonthrowing elbow down and back, rotate your hips and shoulders, throw, and follow through so that your throwing hand finishes at your opposite hip pocket.

A QUICK RELEASE: You have to look at other people as you advance from one level to the next, to get an idea of what you want to do as a passer. And it's okay to emulate other people. But eventually, if you're going to get to the highest level, you have to have your own style of throwing the football and believe in what you're doing. I really believe I always had my own style. All the fundamentals are still the same. That's always got to be there. But, it's something you develop and you get a feel for what works for you.

I think one of the reasons that I've been pretty accurate is that I have a very compact throwing motion and I use my body a lot. There are times when I will throw just with my arm, when I have to. But most of the time I don't take a long step in my throwing motion. I've learned to shorten my step with my front foot and use a lot of my hips and my legs in my throw. I think that's one of the reasons why my delivery is fairly quick.

—Dan Marino
Quarterback, Miami Dolphins

about 20 to 25 feet away from a flat, smooth (brick or masonry) wall. (Adjust the distance for young players.) Using the wall as your target, do a three-step drop, and throw the ball at the wall, as if you were hitting a receiver five yards or so down the field.

If thrown properly, the ball will fly with the nose slightly up and to the right (for a right-handed passer). When it hits the wall and bounces off, it will travel down and to the left (1). For lefties, the

throwing the football

Figure 5.14a   Figure 5.14b   Figure 5.14c

Figure 5.14d   Figure 5.14e   Figure 5.14f

Figure 5.14g   Figure 5.14h   Figure 5.14i

> The five-step drop gives you a little more depth in the pocket for deeper timing routes and for throwing long. Get off the line just as you do on the three-step drop so that your right foot lands directly away from center, with your front shoulder pointed downfield. You should be looking at the whole field. Your second step off the line is a crossover step and so is your fourth. So on the five-step drop, you step, cross over, step, cross over, and land. If the route you throw to is a timing pattern, you'll push the ball back, land, and throw. If you throw long, then you'll add a slide-and-gather step, moving back toward the line to put more power on the ball. If you throw long, remember to look up above your receiver so that you throw the ball with an upward trajectory.

ball will bounce to the right and down (2). Throw a spiral with some zip. Don't lob it. That's why I say move in closer for younger children.

Down and to the left (righties) tells you that you're getting the right push on the ball with your index finger. That's what makes the ball travel with the nose slightly up.

Now, let's say the ball bounces up left or right instead of down (4 and 3). That probably means that your wrist is cocked over too far and that you're late spinning the ball as you release. The nose is traveling with a slightly downward pitch. So when it hits the wall, it bounces up.

The other common bounce that you often see is down and to the right. Now for a left-handed passer, that's perfectly normal. Think about it. The pusher finger for a lefty is pushing in and down, which sets the attitude of the ball (its angle of flight) nose up and to the left. The ball is also spinning in the opposite direction of a football thrown by a right-handed passer. So the ball bounces down and to the right when it hits the wall. The football will also go down and right when it's thrown by a righty if the passer rotates his wrist the wrong way as he releases and spins the ball. Instead of pronating the wrist so the thumb and palm face down on the follow-through,

throwing the football

Figure 5.15a

Figure 5.15b

Figure 5.15c

Figure 5.15d

Figure 5.15e

Figure 5.15f

Figure 5.15g

Figure 5.15h

Figure 5.15i

Figure 5.15j

Figure 5.15k

Figure 5.15l

Figure 5.15m

Seven-step drops will take you deeper into the pocket to give your receivers time to run maneuver routes and multiple routes. Take your first step away from center so that you open up all the way, but this time turn your shoulders away from the line so that your back is to the defense for your first three steps. Turn and put distance between you and the line. As you take your fourth step, which is a crossover step, turn your left shoulder back toward the line so that your chest faces the sideline and you can see the defense downfield. Your fifth step is a normal step. Number six is a crossover and you land on seven. As you land, look for your primary receiver. Push the ball back with front-hand pressure and throw. If the pattern is deep, you may need a slide-and-gather step to add momentum (Figure 5.15j). Don't rush any part of the drop or the throw. Stay in your normal rhythm: one, two, three, cross over, step, cross over, land, and throw. Or, cross over, land, slide-and-gather, and throw, depending on the depth of the pass.

the player rotates his wrist the opposite way and spins the ball from underneath. He finishes the throw with his palm up and elbow in, unable to follow through. A ball thrown this way often winds up as a duck or a helicopter. Anytime you see a passer throw a duck, you can bet that he finished under the ball, palm up.

COMPENSATION

As you work and learn the fundamentals of throwing the football, you will begin to recognize them in other quarterbacks as you watch them play. You'll also begin to see their errors and bad

throwing the football

Figure 5.16a   **Figure 5.16b**   **Figure 5.16c**

Look at the difference between throwing short and throwing long. Note the angle of the shoulders. For the shorter throw, the eyes are straight ahead and level (Figure 5.16a); the front shoulder is level or little down from level so that it stays down during the throw. The front shoulder is up for the long throw (Figure 5.16b). If you look up and throw the ball upward, it will nose over to the receiver downfield. Try not to let your hips get too far out in front as you step to throw (Figure 5.16c). If they do, you won't be able to get your weight shifted over to your front foot and you'll tend to drop your throwing shoulder under the ball. The ball will start flying upward but then it will tail off and never turn over as it should.

habits. And what you'll notice after a while is most bad habits are the direct result of the body trying to compensate for some variation off of the correct form. Take the knee lockout, for example. I was watching a game with my son the other night, and he pointed out the way a quarterback was locking out his knee on every throw. I mean he did it every time. So we started keeping track of all the secondary effects that grew out of that one basic error.

When he locked out his knee, he would hold onto the ball a little longer so he could manipulate it as he threw his body forward to generate power. His delivery was very rushed and jerky, and he threw a lot of balls into the ground. His receivers had a terrible time catching his short passes because he was throwing the ball so hard. He had to throw hard to get the ball to fly at all. The more we watched him, the more we could see that everything he did was to compensate for the lockout. His whole throwing motion

Figure 5.17a

Figure 5.17b

Figure 5.17c

Figure 5.17d

Look at the shoulder and hip rotation on this throw. The front shoulder starts perpendicular to the line of scrimmage. As you push off your back foot and drive your left elbow down and back, your shoulders and hips should rotate nearly 180 degrees as you complete the throw and follow-through.

was a flawed chain reaction of bad habits because of one fundamental mistake. And it hurt him. It affected his accuracy and his touch on the ball.

Among young quarterbacks it's throwing long that will often bring out the worst in their mechanics. They pitch their hips too far forward. Their back arm and shoulder drop. To generate any force on the pass, they have to manipulate the ball with the hand. When they drop the arm and the hand gets underneath, they usually finish the throwing motion with the palm up and with no follow-through. And you know what happens next: ducks and helicopters. The football wobbles through the air or spins sideways. Every time you see a kid throw a duck, you should know

throwing the football

Figure 5.18a   Figure 5.18b   Figure 5.18c

Figure 5.18d   Figure 5.18e   Figure 5.18f

Figure 5.18g   Figure 5.18h   Figure 5.18i

> Landing on your last step of a five-step drop, keep your weight concentrated on the inside portion of the ball of your back foot and knee. Keep your front shoulder pointed downfield and your toes to the sideline. Hold the football in both hands, high in front of your chest. As you step to throw, land heel-toe on your front foot, just outside the plane of your shoulder, toward your intended receiver. Push off your back foot and drive your nonthrowing elbow down and back. Your throwing arm will lag a little behind as your hips and shoulders rotate through the throwing motion and the follow-through to your opposite hip. Notice how the hips and shoulders remain parallel throughout the throwing motion.

that he stopped his motion somewhere in the middle. If you throw with the proper mechanics, you really can't stop the correct throwing motion. It happens naturally. You might not throw a perfect spiral every time, but the ball will not fly like a duck.

There will be pressured times when you'll need to get rid of the ball any way you possibly can. But under normal conditions you don't want to have to manipulate the ball with your hand. That's where problems begin. When your technique is fundamentally sound, the ball will fly correctly because you've done all the right things. But when you leave something out or you get the steps out of sequence, you have to do something to make up for the lost energy or direction. The point is that you've got to be diligent about your fundamentals. Your body and your mind will compensate for your errors, and you won't often consciously realize what you're doing. Practice and look at yourself with a critical eye in your game tapes. Look at what you're doing wrong, try to find the fundamental cause, and correct it before you develop bad habits that are hard to correct.

WATCH AND LEARN

One thing I am able to do now as a broadcaster is really watch all the quarterbacks in the NFL and observe what they do. I always did that to some extent before, but I guess I have a different, more

throwing the football

Figure 5.19a   Figure 5.19b   Figure 5.19c

Figure 5.19d   Figure 5.19e

Demonstrating the three phases of the throwing motion; cocking the ball into throwing position, accelerating the arm through the throw, and decelerating it in the follow-through. Look at the weight shift from the back foot to the front. Remember, passing the football is a full-body motion. The goal is to create momentum with your body toward your target, harnessing all the energy generated by your legs, hips, and shoulders.

complete perspective now. We have covered many of the fundamentals of passing, but there's a lot to be gained from watching other quarterbacks and really studying what they do. Watch the way the ball flies and where it goes relative to the receiver. Look for the techniques we've covered, and look for the errors we've discussed. If you see a simple ten-yard-out pass go low and fall short of the receiver, look at the instant replay to see if the passer locked out his front knee on the throw. You'll be surprised at how much more you'll begin to see and what you can learn from it.

> **STUDY THE POSITION:** I think it's key for young quarterbacks today to watch other quarterbacks play. They should observe all the high school, college, and professional players they can and try to make a study of the position on their own so that they appreciate it and understand what these other people do. Study them rather than just watch the game as a fan. Then read books like this one, and throw and catch the ball a lot. Maybe you'll hook up with someone who knows the game and who is a teacher rather than just a blustering coach. Make a science of the position. Make a study of it as you observe other quarterbacks pass the football. And do a lot of throwing, all kinds of throwing: long, short, running right, running left, throwing accurately. Accuracy is by far the most important factor for the young quarterback. It's certainly not how hard you throw the ball. It's accuracy, no doubt. The way you build accuracy is by playing a lot of catch and throwing to a target that's moving, and stationary, in addition to drills and things that help to build and reinforce good mechanics.
>
> **—Bill Walsh**
> **Retired Head Coach, Stanford University**
> **Former Head Coach, San Francisco 49ers**

throwing the football

One of the cleanest and most technically correct of the young quarterbacks right now is Erik Kramer of the Chicago Bears. He's almost perfect in just about everything he does. He carries the ball well all the time. His drops are smooth and rhythmic. When he lands on his back foot, he's able to push, turn, rotate his hips, and transfer his weight on every single throw. And though he throws the ball with power and accuracy, it's soft. The ball's not going to knock you over, but he doesn't float it either. He's not working to throw it hard. He just throws with authority. His throwing sequence and mechanics are so good that the ball just comes out at the perfect speed, almost every single throw. I guess, if I could teach my son to throw like any quarterback in the NFL right now, it would be Erik.

The other new guy I like to watch is Jeff Blake from the Cincinnati Bengals. He does some great things when he throws the football. He's got a picture-perfect long ball, a beautiful spiral that he puts out there high, and it just noses over into his receiver's hands. His mechanics are straight out of the Jim Fassel school of quarterbacking. When he drops back, he gets his shoulders perpendicular to the line, toes to the sideline. His head is up and his knees are slightly bent; hips and shoulders are level. And as he throws, he gets all of his weight over his left foot. His left knee stays slightly bent as he steps forward to land heel-toe. That's got to be one of the reasons he is so consistently accurate and has such a good touch on the football. And that's true for both his short and distance throws. This guy is really solid in everything he does with the football and another good example for a young player to observe and emulate.

Among the veterans, you won't find too many who do as many things right as Jim Kelly. Overall, he does a lot of good things. But I don't know if he's ever been taught. Yet you could stop his passing motion just about any time during his sequence and you would always find him in a good position to throw. He has good balance. That's the thing that strikes me when I watch him. When he throws, he's balanced. And when he finishes, he's the same way. He keeps his body centered.

Figure 5.20   What's wrong here? I'm throwing more like a baseball pitcher than a quarterback. The ball is too low and too far away from my body. You want to hold it higher and closer, at your chest, so you can move it smoothly up and back into the cocked position to throw.

throwing the football

He doesn't let himself get too spread out or out of control. I think he's taught himself to be that way. He's had to develop solid mechanics because he plays in such bad weather up there in Buffalo. The cold, the wind, and the rain have conditioned him and refined his skills.

The other guy that always sticks in my mind is Dan Marino. He does so many great things. He slides in the pocket and keeps himself in position to throw. And he throws the ball incredibly well, the best you'll see anybody throw a football. Dan is not known as a scrambler but he can hop around in the pocket and create lanes. He can adjust and give himself that extra half second he needs to throw the ball. Dan always keeps his shoulders parallel to sidelines. He sees the pressure and moves. He keeps his focus and composure, moves out of the way, steps up, and throws the football.

Moreover, he always has a tremendous follow-through. He takes that right shoulder and propels it forward. His hips rotate and his left arm pulls and he just drives that right shoulder forward and makes all the other things happen. That's the reason he is so accurate: his motion is the same every time. You could say he's a shoulder thrower, but he really throws with his whole body. He doesn't try to finesse or manipulate the ball with his hand and his arm. His motion is like a bodily convulsion that just propels the ball forward. I'm sure that's one of the reasons why he can throw the ball so hard and so accurately. People say he has a quick release. He does but it's all his shoulders. There's no long windup. Dan just rotates so hard and fast with his body that the ball is gone with one quick, convulsive motion.

Figure 5.21   Jim Kelly, Buffalo Bills. Jim Kelly is a guy who always seems to be in the right position to pass the football. Toes to the sideline, front shoulder pointed down the field, he's got the ball in both hands, chest high, ready to push it into the cocked position with front-hand pressure so he can throw. Look at his fingers on the ball. He's a two-and-five gripper with his little finger just under the fifth lace. Notice the slight bend to his knees. His back heel is slightly off the ground with his weight concentrated on the inside edge of the ball of his foot and knee. It looks like Jim is just getting ready to step toward his target to throw. As you become more of a student of the position, these are some of the details you want to look out for as you watch other quarterbacks play at all levels.

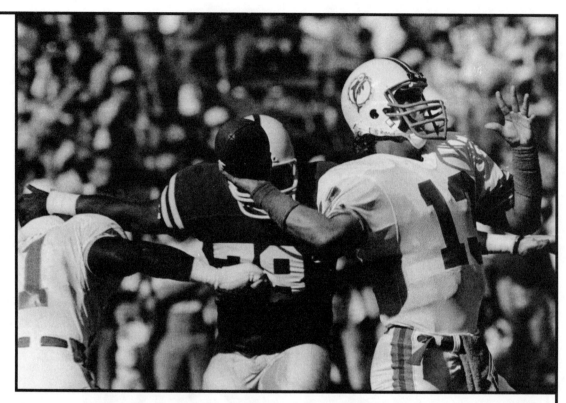

Figure 5.22   Dan Marino, Miami Dolphins. It's difficult to illustrate in still pictures but Dan Marino's passing motion is very quick. He definitely has his own style but it's solidly based in strong fundamentals. His short first step and quick delivery is a very compact but full body motion. Look at the position of his throwing arm when it's cocked and ready to throw. You can see the power in his shoulder and arm as they are poised and ready to fire. His nonthrowing arm is in position to drive down and back to initiate his shoulder rotation in the throw.

We've covered a lot of the essential mechanics of throwing: the push off the back foot, pulling the opposite arm back, the hip rotation, the shoulders and the arm motion. Then sometimes I look at Dan and I wonder if his shoulder makes all the other things happen, if his right shoulder brings his right hip forward and causes all the other correct things to happen. Even though some of the particulars may seem out of order, the end result is that Dan's body is moving forward as he throws. He's using all the momentum generated by his forward motion to propel the football forward.

Figure 5.23   Now look at the slight bend in Dan's front knee after he's released the football. His hips and shoulders are rotated. He's transferred his weight to his front foot and you can see that his arm was slightly lagging as the ball left his hand.

throwing the football

Figure 5.24 John Elway, Denver Broncos. John Elway puts everything he has into his passes with an extremely efficient throwing motion. There's nothing in his technique that works against the transfer of power from his legs through his hips and shoulders to the ball. See how his head is slightly tilted to one side as his hips and shoulders rotate through the delivery. His arm lags slightly as it whips forward, transferring a tremendous amount of power to the football.

I don't know if you could ever teach anybody to throw like Dan. I wish I could, but my thought is that he has a God-given talent that's unique to him. I've had the chance to broadcast a couple of his games this year, and I've seen him turn in some great performances. We even watched him work out in practice, and he threw the ball just as quick and hard.

John Elway is another powerful passer who commands everyone's respect. His delivery is different from Marino's. It looks a little longer because he gets his whole body moving forward before his arm reacts, which is good. That's one of the reasons why he can throw it so far. He has tremendous quickness and tremendous power in his body to begin with. When he throws and gets his arm lagging behind his body, it just whips through as it rushes forward to launch the ball. That's one of the reasons he can throw it so hard and so far. It may look like a long motion compared to Marino's, but it happens fast. It's one of the best examples of the whipping motion you want in your passing arm.

If you really want to study the position and see the importance of the fundamentals we've discussed, watch these guys play. Study their mechanics, and think about what they do as you work during in the off-season to improve your skills. As you watch any quarterback play, if he throws a few passes into the ground, short of a receiver or over his head, look at the instant replay if it's on TV, or watch him throw for the rest of the game and see if you can determine what's happening, where his mechanics may be breaking down. Look at yourself on tape with a critical eye and work to improve your technique. As you get older and advance in the sport, you'll find that this kind of self-motivated skill development is what separates the average from the outstanding performer.

throwing the football

CHAPTER 6

Sprint-out Passing

Figure 6.0   What's wrong this time? Both feet are pointed toward the line of scrimmage.
My shoulders are half turned to the line. Early in my career a lot of what I did was guesswork. Sometimes I'd get it right and sometimes I'd get it half right. Somehow, I'd get it
out there.

I was never much of a sprint-out passer during most of my career. For one thing, the Giants didn't run that kind of an offense while I was there. I guess they could have if I had been more effective at it, but I had a problem overthrowing the receiver when I sprinted out. After Jim Fassel started working with me, I got fairly good at it, but it was pretty clear that my future was not going to depend on the sprint-out pass.

Before then, I never really understood the mechanics of it. I always believed in the long-held myth that sprint-outs were different from drop-back passes. I had been taught, like every other quarterback I knew at the time, that you were supposed to throw off the opposite foot. A right-handed passer who normally threw off his right foot (that's your back foot) would now throw off of his left. That was the way every clinic I ever attended taught the sprint-out pass.

After I understood the correct mechanics, I thought about why my sprint-outs were always high and it made pretty good sense. The way I was throwing, my left knee was locked straighter than a board. And because I was running as I threw, I couldn't get my upper body over the top to compensate. My shoulders were out of whack, and my hips were in the wrong position. So I threw a lot of balls that I thought were going to be right on target. But more often than not, they ended up a full arm's length too high and rising fast.

I remember Jeff Hostetler and I laughed after Jim showed us the right way to do it. We picked up the technique right away and it was easy because it was such a natural and coordinated motion. Another great myth was laid to rest.

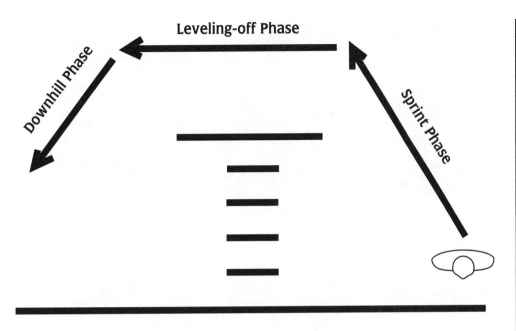

Figure 6.1   Three phases of the sprint-out pass

THREE PHASES

The whole idea behind sprint-out passing is to get the quarterback out of the pocket and to the perimeter to throw the football. To do that effectively, you've got to get away from the line of scrimmage and get depth equivalent to a five-step drop. Then you've got to get outside the tackle toward the sideline. And finally, you want to be moving toward your target when you throw, which means you need to move back toward the line of scrimmage just before you release the ball. It all breaks down into three distinct phases: the sprint phase, the leveling-off phase, and the downhill phase (Figure 6.1).

Sprint

The sprint-out is intended to do one thing: get you off the line as quickly as possible (Figure 6.2). It begins with a step 45 degrees away from center. Remember to take a pigeon-toed stance to avoid any wasted motion.

sprint-out passing

| Figure 6.2a | Figure 6.2b | Figure 6.2c |

| Figure 6.2d | Figure 6.2e | Figure 6.2f |

As you turn, bring the football up to midchest, with your elbows in and shoulders relaxed. Point your shoulders in the direction you want to run and take off. Just turn and run. Remember, running with your elbows in will keep your arm swing to a minimum as you move and give you better control of the football.

Keep the ball close to you, without resting it against your body, and run for about seven to eight yards. Stay loose and run as fast as you can. Quickly put as much distance as you can between you and the defense.

Leveling-off

As you reach the full depth of your sprint (seven to eight yards), it's time to level off and cut your speed to about 75 percent

Figure 6.3a

Figure 6.3b

Figure 6.3c

Figure 6.3d

Figure 6.3e

(Figure 6.3). Get yourself under control and reduce your body lean, but maintain a full stride. You're not running full speed anymore but you still need to cover ground. Carry the ball chest high with elbows in and shoulders loose. Your shoulders should be square to the sideline at this point, with your head still facing downfield, reading the defense and your receivers.

Downhill

After about five yards, start your move back toward the line of scrimmage to pass by squaring your hips with your target, the point on the field where you anticipate throwing the ball (Figure 6.4). I'm not talking about the receiver. I mean the place you expect you expect the receiver will be when he catches it.

sprint-out passing

Figure 6.4a

Figure 6.4b

Figure 6.4c

Figure 6.4d

Figure 6.4e

Figure 6.4f

Figure 6.4g

Cut your speed some more now to get yourself totally under control. Shorten your stride and raise your body up a little. When I say shorten your stride, I mean chop it. Don't shuffle your feet. That might cause you to stumble. Lift your feet but take short, choppy steps. Lean forward a little with your body. This will help you get rid of the ball quickly.

Long strides can get you stuck in the middle of a big step when you see your chance to throw. The tendency for many quarterbacks in this situation is to take one more long stride to get their feet in position and then lean back and throw. That's a lot of wasted motion, and it can eat up time you don't have. Moreover, your body is not in a good position to throw the ball. You will very likely lose speed and accuracy on the throw, either of which can result in an interception. With your body up a little (chest up, head erect), with short choppy steps and a little forward body lean, your body is in a much better position to deliver the football. One short step and you are ready to throw.

Two important things should happen when you pass the ball. First, you want to have the same foot forward and the same foot on the ground as you would if you were setting up to throw in the pocket. A lot of players think you should do just the opposite and throw through the step. In fact, a right-handed passer will get more power with his left foot forward and his right foot on the ground. He doesn't have to muscle the ball to the target with his arm. The real secret is rising up a little so you're in a better position to throw. If the receiver breaks and you happen to be on the wrong foot, you take one more short step and fire away.

Second, the throwing motion is more like the flick of a dart than a pass. You can't wind up when you throw the ball on the run. You haven't got the time. So you have to deliver the ball with a short snap of the wrist from no farther back than the ear hole of your helmet.

Remember, you've still got the ball in two hands when you finish the leveling-off phase. As you start the downhill phase, a little front-hand pressure and a short rotation of the shoulders will quickly move the ball up a little and back toward the throwing position. For me that's just below the shoulder. Continue to carry the ball with both hands. The temptation will be to release your front hand and carry the ball with your passing hand alone, but don't do it. Find the place that's

sprint-out passing

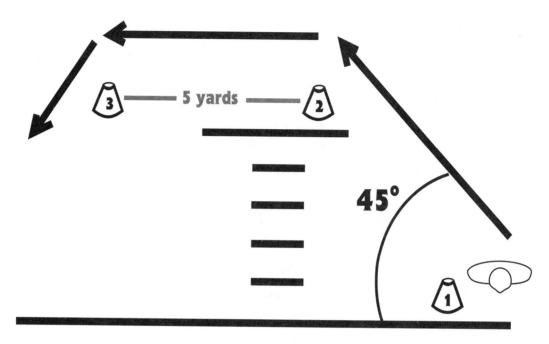

Figure 6.5

comfortable for you and stick with both hands until the moment you're ready to throw. Remember to keep your shoulders loose and your elbows in for better mobility. The combination of your quick throwing motion and the momentum of your body will generate the force you need on the ball. Just step and flick the ball. You're not throwing a seam route. This is a short pattern with a quick break. To complete it, you need a quick, accurate delivery.

RUNNING THE CONES

One of the best ways I know to practice the sprint-out motion is to set up plastic cones at the transition points of the three phases. Again, for simplicity we'll set up cones for a right-handed passer. You don't need a center. Instead, to mark your starting point place a cone where the center would be. If you've got them, it's also a good idea to set out cones to define the ends of the offensive line, one on each end (Figure 6.5).

Now place another cone behind your imaginary line of scrimmage, about eight yards from the center cone at a 45-degree angle. This pair of cones will mark the sprint phase. Set your next cone about five yards away from the cone marking the end of the sprint phase, toward the sideline.

A line drawn between the second and third cone should be parallel to your imaginary line of scrimmage. This pair of cones defines the leveling-off phase of the sprint-out. This last cone also signals the beginning of the downhill phase. Start the drill in a good quarterback position, as if you were under center at the center cone. Remember: on the balls of your feet, knees bent, pigeon-toed, bottom-hand pressure, back straight, head erect. From this position you should be able to step out at a 45-degree angle and sprint hard for the second cone.

Get your shoulders around quickly and point them at the second cone. Make sure you're carrying the ball with two hands, chest high, elbows in, and shoulders loose. As you round the second cone, cut your speed to 75 percent, and look downfield. Continue at full stride until you get to the third cone and begin to turn back toward the line. As you begin this downhill phase of the drill, cut your speed further, begin to chop your steps, and look for your receiver. Raise your body up a little and, as you get closer to the point where you're going to pass the ball, initiate a little forward lean. (Just slightly; don't put yourself off-balance.) In this position you can deliver the ball in a fraction of a second. Practice cocking the football quickly and throwing with

sprint-out passing

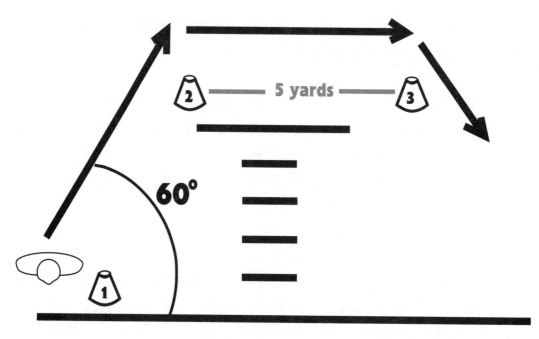

Figure 6.6

a dartlike throwing motion. The key is rising up a little and taking short, choppy steps so you can quickly position your feet to throw.

A STEEPER ANGLE

Figure 6.6 shows a steeper angle to the first cone. We've been describing a sprint-out to the right for a right-handed passer. What about a sprint-out to the left, for a righty quarterback? Any differences? Yes, and it's a major one.

Coming off the line of scrimmage during the sprint phase, you want to angle your first step a little more than 45 degrees so you can get deep faster (Figure 6.7); 55 to 60 degrees is probably okay. Experiment to see what kind of an angle will get you deep enough so that by the time you're ready to level off, you get your shoulders more squared up to the line.

Figure 6.7a

Figure 6.7b

Figure 6.7c

Figure 6.7d

Figure 6.7e

The leveling-off phase to this side angles back to the line of scrimmage more so you don't have to throw the ball across your body (Figure 6.8). As a right-handed quarterback, moving to my right, it's a lot easier for me to adjust and throw across my body to the right because my shoulders are naturally squared up on my target.

Figure 6.8a

Figure 6.8b

Figure 6.8c

sprint-out passing

Figure 6.9a

Figure 6.9b

Figure 6.9c

Figure 6.9d

Figure 6.9e

To throw a sprint-out to the left, I have to rotate my shoulders to the right more to get my body behind the pass (Figure 6.9). If I don't, my body and shoulders would essentially be moving left as I'm trying to throw the ball to my right. The momentum of my body would be directed at a different angle than the one in which I'm trying to throw. The result is loss of power on the ball.

As we said earlier, a steeper angle from the line allows you to get deep and squared around quickly so you can level off and come back at the line to pass at a steeper angle, with your shoulders at a better angle to throw the ball with power. Your momentum is behind the ball now, as you dart pass it to your receiver downfield.

COMMON MISTAKES

Standing up too tall is probably the most common error that quarterbacks make as they move outside the pocket to throw the ball.

They rise up as high as they can to see what's going on and they take their body out of position to throw the ball. In doing that they tend to narrow their base a bit too much. Their knees are straight, and they tend to square their shoulders too much with the line of scrimmage.

A sprint-out passer should rise up a little but not so much that he's on the balls of his feet and his knees are straight. In this position you almost have to lean back and cock the ball more than usual to get any power on it. Leaning back brings your front shoulder up. Throwing in this position, you're bound either to float one over your receiver's hands or to bury one at his feet, depending on whether or not you try to muscle the ball to the target. Remember, even when you're throwing on the move, you still want to keep your front shoulder down and your knees slightly bent. Rising up a little gives you a little more range of motion for your arm and a little more leverage on the ball as you flick it out there like a dart. One doesn't preclude the other. You can rise up a little and still keep your shoulder down and your knees slightly bent.

SCRAMBLE PASS

Another pass that Jim introduced to us when he was with the Giants was the scramble pass. Some people call it a dash. Whatever you call it, you take the ball from center, drop back, and then sprint out toward the sideline and stop again, then set up and throw as if you were in the pocket.

When we started working on it, I was amazed at the bad habits that came out. I did things when I set up outside the pocket that were technically very bad. I wouldn't get into a good throwing position as I should have. I'd stand straight up and be looking

sprint-out passing

129

around like a turkey. We had four quarterbacks at the time and everybody would do the same thing. It's just a natural instinct, I guess, to forget about keeping your knees slightly bent and your toes to the sideline. So we started working on it. We'd get out there, set up in good throwing position, and make sure we had our weight centered the way we were supposed to. We'd work at being ready to push off the back foot and keeping the front knee bent and our hips and shoulders level.

The scramble pass is sort of a combination sprint-out and drop-back pass. But don't kid yourself into thinking that because you can drop back and sprint out that the combination will be easy. Practice it as a distinct passing technique. Drop back, sprint to the outside, stop, and get into a good drop-back passing position to throw the football.

THROWING ON THE RUN

The big difference between sprint-out passing and throwing on the run is planning. The sprint-out is a choreographed move to the perimeter to deliver the ball in three distinct phases. Throwing on the run is just that. It's that tense situation where you've got four down linemen and at least two linebackers chasing you out of the pocket and you've got to get the pass off. So you run and look for your best shot.

The key to throwing on the run is that anything goes. I've seen quarterbacks throw behind their back, over their shoulder, underhand, sidearm—you name it and some desperate quarterback has tried it. Jim Fassel used to say that you know it's going to happen sooner or later, so practice for it. Practice throwing the ball while you're scrambling. Run the pocket or wave drill, where you're moving

Figure 6.10   Sometimes you have to throw off-balance.

sprint-out passing

Figure 6.11   Moving toward the sideline, I've got to throw across my body because I'm on the run. This is a great example of why, in addition to the basics, it's important for you to practice throwing the ball any way you can. Work at scrambling, moving, and tossing the ball so that these kinds of skills are automatic when you're under pressure.

around in the pocket, and then just throw the ball from wherever you are: on the heels, across your body, behind your back, whatever. Try to get your body moving toward your target when you can, but most important, get the ball off and get used to doing it spontaneously.

Throw it hard, throw it soft, or loft it so it will float over a defender's head. Use your imagination. Teach yourself to have a little feel in those challenging situations. Make it up as you would when you're practicing your inside basketball moves and you must put the ball in the basket any way you can. Visualize the situation, and get the pass off any way you can (Figure 6.10).

Pro golfers have a technique they use when their body is out of position on a shot. Many of them let go of the club with one hand so they can keep the ball on the golf course. It takes a certain touch that they develop over time. The same is true with pro quarterbacks. They develop a feeling for getting the ball to the receiver when they're in the wrong position to throw. But a young player will not have that feel unless he's extremely gifted.

As you progress, there are a number of qualities that coaches will use to judge your effectiveness as a quarterback: how far you can throw, how accurate you are, the way you move with the ball, and so on. Another one of those important qualities they'll be looking for as you play at higher levels is how well you adapt and improvise under pressure, how well you throw from various angles and positions. In a NFL game, against today's defensive players, if you throw thirty passes, you're going to throw five or six of them under serious pressure. You're going to throw sidearm, off your back foot, sideways, across your body, and running forward (Figure 6.11). You're going to have to be able to do that.

And you can practice it. I worked at it. After doing all my warm-ups and drills properly, I would take about ten throws where I'd run right, for example, and just sling it almost underhanded. I'd just whip it or I'd run left and throw it back the other way or stop as

sprint-out passing

Figure 6.12   You may have to rise up a little higher sometimes or do whatever it takes to get over the top, knowing there's pressure coming in from other directions. Sometimes you can feel the pressure, sometimes you can't. A quick release will get the ball away and a relaxed body will help you avoid injury or the hit...even a blind one. Solid fundamentals will ensure both.

fast as I could and bend low, as if I were ducking a tackler, and throw one. I'd jump and throw a couple of balls. I'd practice those every day. I'd throw them sidearm—I mean really sidearm, like someone was in my way and I couldn't see over him. I'd dip below, look down and sling it upward. I'd rise up and throw (Figure 6.12). I'd throw every way I could imagine. Jim Fassel used to do work with us. We'd work on all of our mechanics, do all of our drills, and then he'd tell us to drop back and just run and throw it somewhere, just sling it. He deliberately worked at getting us used to throwing at different angles. And like all the other little things he introduced into our technique, it paid off in clutch situations during the games and seasons that followed.

sprint-out passing

CHAPTER 7

A Quarterback's Workout

Figure 7.0   Under control. First step off the line: The ball is up at my chest
and my shoulders are parallel with the sideline. My hands and my arms are
relaxed and I'm looking downfield.

I started lifting weights after my senior year in high school after football season was over. I didn't play basketball that year. I weighed about 175 or 180 pounds, and I wanted to play college football. So I knew that I needed to get a little bigger. I hadn't done any serious training like that before, so I could see results almost immediately. As I got bigger and stronger, I could also see the direct result in my athletic play. My speed picked up right away. My legs were stronger, and my coordination improved.

The results felt good, and I was hooked. So the lifting carried on through my college career and into the pros. But weight lifting for quarterbacks wasn't the accepted practice in the NFL at the time, and I really didn't know all that I could do to protect myself and improve my performance. After I got hurt a couple of times, I was willing to do anything to try to stay healthy. And that's when I became convinced that I needed to add a little muscle, to tighten up and to absorb the impact of incoming tacklers.

Coaches were concerned that the lifting might adversely affect my throwing motion. But I wasn't lifting for bulk. I wasn't trying to add eighty pounds of muscle. I just did what I could to stay strong. Then, in the spring of 1994, Johnny Parker came to the Giants, and we started doing some serious lifting as part of an organized program of weight training.

During the off-season we went four times a week. It was extremely hard work. We went four times a week during the season, too, but the workouts were not quite as intense. They were still pretty challenging, though. I noticed a big difference in myself, both in the way I felt and played. But that's not all. Training hard does a lot of things for you. The game of football is about being tough, no matter what position you play. And when you train hard, it'll make you tough. Advanced training can be brutal. And believe me, the mentality it takes to get through it carries over to the football field. And it's just as important as the physical effects. The more accustomed you get to doing the hard work and taking a little punishment, the tougher you play. It was good for us, and I believe it had a direct result on game day.

RESPONSIVENESS

This may sound a little strange, but one of the best ways I've heard anyone describe the action of a quarterback's throwing arm is to compare it to a bicycle chain. If the chain is too loose, the bike hesitates when you push down on the pedal until one of the links catches on a gear tooth. You don't want that. When you push down on the pedal, you want an instant response from the bike. The same is true of your throwing arm. When you go to throw the ball, the muscles in your shoulder and arm should respond instantly and not hesitate. They must be tight and conditioned but elastic. When you want your arm to come forward to throw, it must come forward immediately. There can't be any hesitation in it, as there would be in a loose chain.

That's why you want to lift weights. You want to build responsiveness in the muscle. You want to build endurance and power. You want to prevent injury and to make your performance better. Those are the keys. I found weight lifting was a great help throughout my career, especially for preventing injury. Think about all the hits you take in the shoulder as a quarterback, the falls and times you brace yourself with your arm. It helps to have muscle tissue that keeps the shoulder joint tight and provides some padding for the bones.

a quarterback's workout

The trick is finding the right level of conditioning. I'm not saying you should look like Arnold Schwarzenegger. You don't want bulk that can interfere with your athletic performance. And you don't want to get too tight. I guess you could say the goal of weight conditioning for a quarterback is to increase the strength of the muscles around the joint and therefore increase the stability of the shoulder. But the shoulder joint is the most complex joint in the body. It's supported by sixteen different muscles. It has the largest range of motion in the body. It moves in almost every direction. That means the conditioning you do to build and increase muscle tone throughout the joint will have to be done from all directions: front, side, and back, always encouraging full range of motion. No one exercise or type of weight lifting will do the job. It will take a combination exercises to attack each muscle group effectively.

Figure 7.1a　　　　　　**Figure 7.1b**

Bench presses (Figure 7.1) are one of the best ways to build the muscles in the front of the shoulder. You should use a straight bar, lifting it directly above the chest and bringing it straight down, with a slight pause at the bottom—about a second—so that the bar touches your chest lightly. Don't rest the bar on your chest or bounce it either. Just touch and take the bar straight up.

At the top of the lift, be careful no to lock out your elbows. Take the bar up so that you end the lift just a few degrees short of lockout at the elbows—about half an inch away. Start off light, at a comfortable weight that will allow you to do three sets of eight to ten lifts. As you continue your workouts, gradually increase the weight. Don't rush it. The key word here is gradual. Take your time and make steady progress toward a long-term goal, which in this case should be to gain the strength to bench press the equivalent of your body weight at least five times.

Figure 7.2a

Figure 7.2b

Dumbbell bench presses (Figure 7.2) are a more advanced form of the straight bar press. They are also very effective in strengthening the front or anterior muscles of the shoulder. But they should be done only after you've built up some base strength with the straight-bar presses. Dumbbell presses make use of and require greater range of motion and stability in the joint because they involve more surrounding muscles as you lift. You not only involve the muscles that allow you to take the weights straight up and down, but you also recruit muscles that keep the separate weights in balance and control. Use dumbbell presses to add variety to your workout and to build greater range of motion in the shoulder.

a quarterback's workout

Again, your workout should include three sets of eight to ten repetitions. The total weight of both dumbbells should not exceed 50 to 70 percent of what your straight-bar lifting weight is. So if you're lifting a hundred pounds with the straight-bar, then your dumbbells should not be more than twenty-five to thirty-five pounds each. Remember, start light. Don't rush yourself.

As with the straight bar, you don't want to lock your elbows out at the top of your lift and you don't want to go to far at the bottom either. Try to bring the dumbbells straight down just slightly lower than you brought the straight bar—about an inch farther.

Figure 7.3a   Figure 7.3b

The other dumbbell press that's very effective is the **shoulder press** (Figure 7.3). It's good for working all the muscles of the shoulder, especially the middle ones. In this case, you're seated with your back against the back of the bench. Your feet should be flat on the ground. Begin by holding the dumbbells up so that they are no lower than the bottom of your ears. You don't want to take them any lower during the exercise because it can cause unnecessary stress on the joint. When you raise the dumbbells, be careful not to lock your elbows out at the top of the lift. Here again, you want to do three sets of ten. Ten repetitions is a good number because it builds endurance and strength. It will also build a little bit of muscle mass, but that's not the main goal. You're really getting the best of all worlds.

Figure 7.4a

Figure 7.4b

Another lift that you do seated is the **inclined bench press** (Figure 7.4). But in this exercise you're not sitting up. Your upper body is at about a forty-five-degree angle from the seat of the bench. Pressing a straight bar from this angle recruits more muscle from higher in the chest than the normal bench press you do from a reclined position. So you're targeting muscles that connect at the front of the joint, but from a slightly different angle.

You should also try to alter your grip on the bar slightly as you do these presses. Sometimes I'll grip the bar a little wider, sometimes a little narrower. The idea here is to alter the angle of the exercise slightly to recruit more muscle fibers and to keep from repeating the same exact movement every time. The body gets used to repeating the same exact motion every time, and the exercise isn't quite as effective as it is when you change it slightly. Remember, when you lift weight, the exercise never uses all the muscle available. At best, you're working maybe 40 percent. When you lift a weight in a specific direction and repeat that exact motion, you work only the muscles that produce that movement in that direction and very little around it. When you change the grip or the lift angle slightly, you change the direction of stress on the muscle slightly and involve different muscle fibers in the exercise.

a quarterback's workout

A with the flat bench press, be careful not to lock out your elbows at the top of your lift. A few degrees, or about half an inch off of straight, is plenty. On the bottom end, the bar should just touch your upper chest as you hold for a second before you extend your arms again. Again, don't bounce the weight off your chest and don't rest it either. Just touch for a count and go.

Take it slow. Don't rush through any of these workouts. As you push the weight out away from your body, slowly count to yourself: one, two. And as you let the weight back down, do it on a slow four count: one, two, three, four.

So far, we've hit the front and middle muscles in a couple of different ways. A good exercise that targets the muscles in the back of the shoulder joint is the **bent-over lateral raise**. Now, besides supporting the shoulder joint in its normal range of motion, the muscles that you'll work in this exercise are instrumental in slowing down or stopping the throwing motion as you release the ball and follow through. A lot of injuries occur from not training these muscles enough. We spend a lot of time working the muscles in the front of the shoulder that accelerate the ball to the target. You need to spend equal time developing the decelerating muscle group that relates to the shoulder; that slows the arm down after you release the ball. The overhand throwing motion that you use in pitching a baseball or throwing a football requires good development in the shoulder muscles on the back side of the joint to help prevent injury. Without it, you run the risk of doing serious damage to the rotator cuff muscles, which are smaller muscles surrounding the joint, holding it together and providing stability. Without the larger muscles to decelerate or slow down the arm, the overhand throwing motion can put too much stress on these smaller muscles and tear them.

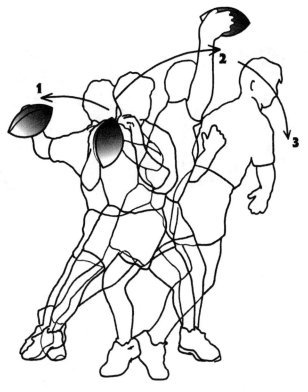

Figure 7.5

Think about what happens when you throw the ball. The throwing motion is divided up into three phases: the wind-up or cocking phase, the acceleration phase, and the deceleration phase or follow-through (Figure 7.5). The rotator cuff and five other surrounding muscle groups all function together to accomplish this action (Figure 7.6). The muscles in the front of the joint contract and pull the arm forward. The stronger and more developed those muscles are, the more velocity the arm gains in the throwing motion.

Once you release the ball, what is there to slow down and stop the arm? The muscle groups that connect to the back of the joint. Muscles in this group contract near the end of the throw or pull it back the other way and slow the arm down. It just stands to

a quarterback's workout

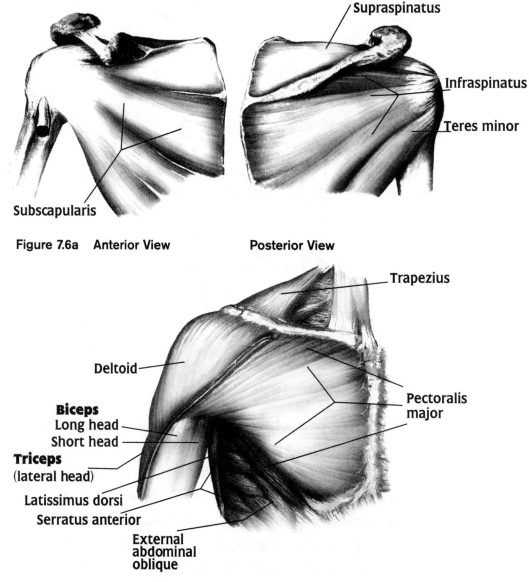

Figure 7.6a   Anterior View   Posterior View

Figure 7.6b   Anterior View

reason, then, that they should be as developed as the ones which pull the arm forward. Without enough conditioned large muscle to slow the arm down, the momentum of the throwing motion can put excessive stress on the support muscles that make up the rotator cuff. I'm sure you've read about baseball pitchers who have had to undergo surgery to repair damage to the rotator cuff.

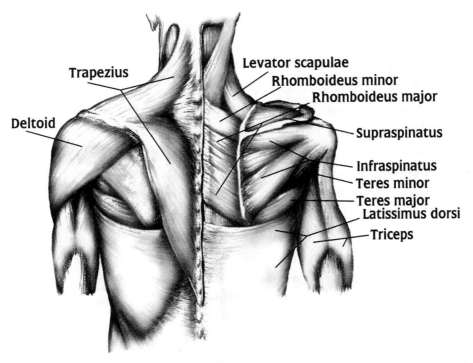

Trapezius

Deltoid

Levator scapulae
Rhomboideus minor
Rhomboideus major
Supraspinatus
Infraspinatus
Teres minor
Teres major
Latissimus dorsi
Triceps

Figure 7.6c

There's no way that these smaller muscles can stand up against the physical stress of a vigorous and repeated overhand throwing motion. They don't have the mass and they don't have the leverage on the joint to do any more than support it. So it's clear: You've got to develop these posterior shoulder muscles to the same level of strength and endurance as all the others in order to ensure balance among the muscles involved in throwing.

If I ever had problems in throwing, it never was getting the arm going forward, whipping it forward. It was stopping my arm. When I got sore, it was always in the back of my shoulder. And not until my last couple of years, when I really started learning more about conditioning, did I stop having that problem—when I started building up the back of my shoulders better. In all the weight training I did up until that time, it was always focused on the front. We

a quarterback's workout

SHOULDER ANATOMY

The muscles that converge at the shoulder that are responsible for its function are usually described in three groups, indicating their location on the front, side, or back of the joint. They are the anterior, middle, and posterior muscles of the shoulder. The deltoid muscle furnishes the primary motor power for the shoulder and the glenohumeral joint. The latissimus dorsi is important to help extend the shoulder and can assist the posterior deltoid muscle with this motion. The anterior deltoid is important for use of the arm in front of the body and the middle deltoid assists the supraspinatus muscle in raising the arm out to the side.

The deltoid, trapezius, and pectoralis major generate powerful movement of the shoulder. The rotator cuff muscles also perform two major functions in this regard. They supply concentric contraction for propulsive movement, that is, muscle contraction that helps to bring the arm forward when throwing. They also provide eccentric contraction for balance of muscle function and help achieve shoulder joint stability. Eccentric contraction is contraction of the cuff muscles to resist the forces of the forward propulsive movement of the arm and slow it down in the follow-through stage. In addition to the deltoid and rotator cuff muscles, the suspensory muscles of the upper extremity, the trapezius and levator scapulae as well as the rhomboids, are all important in providing scapulothoracic motion, which in conjunction with glenohumeral joint movement is necessary for proper throwing mechanics.

ROTATOR CUFF

The rotator cuff is made up of four muscles: the supraspinatus, infraspinatus, subscapularis, and the teres minor. Generally, these four muscles and tendons help to stabilize the joint, generate precision movement and nutrition. More specifically, the supraspinatus functions as a stabilizer of the shoulder joint, which in turn helps the deltoid to work more effectively. The infraspinatus and the teres minor are the primary external rotators of the shoulder, whereas the subscapularis is an internal rotator. External and internal rotation refer to motions of the shoulder and arm away from the body (external) or motions of the shoulder and arm toward the body (internal).

worked on developing the muscle groups in the front of the shoulder. I always worked on getting my arm going forward quickly and with velocity, not stopping it. Of course, you live and learn. I know better now. Forget about that myth that quarterbacks shouldn't lift. That is ancient history. And people are waking up to it.

You have to weight train: to prevent injury, to recover faster, and to raise your performance level. And it works. I proved over a long period of time that weight training does boost your performance.

Bent-over lateral raises (Figure 7.7) are just what they sound like. Sit on the end of the bench so your feet are flat on the floor. Now lean forward with your upper body so that your chest is flat across your thighs and your arms hang down on either side, outside your legs. Take one dumbbell in each hand, and raise each

a quarterback's workout

Figure 7.7a

Figure 7.7b

outward at the same time, with your elbows bent a little less than halfway. Raise them as far as you can comfortably go and return them again to the lowered position at your ankles. Take your time and work light: two count up and four count down. Like the other exercises, you want to do three sets of ten.

In addition to conditioning the gross muscles that support the back of the shoulder joint, I also like to do another exercise that targets the four smaller muscles of the rotator cuff. A lot of injuries occur when these muscles are weak and the joint is loose. The head of the bone that makes up the upper arm, called the humerus bone, can actually pop upward if the stress is severe enough and the rotator cuff muscles are weak. This popping and looseness can cause inflammation and pain in the joint and its surrounding tissues.

Figure 7.8a

Figure 7.8b

Pull-ups (Figure 7.8) are another great exercise that are easy to do and very effective in building overall body strength and balance. Especially when you do front chins. I'm not talking about pull-ups where the bar goes behind your head. The ones that are most effective for our purposes involve pulling your body up so your chin is over the bar.

We've covered a number of exercises that involve pushing a weight over a certain distance. It's important in completing a balanced fitness program that you also involve some pulling exercises. After all, throwing the football begins with a pulling motion. If you do it the right way, the way we've been teaching you here, the throwing motion will begin at the arm with a pull at the shoulder to whip the throwing hand and the ball toward your target. When you do pull-ups, you should pull yourself up so that your chin is above the bar and then let yourself down slowly until your arms are fully extended. The slow let-down is just as important as the pull-up part. So take it slow. Let your arms stretch out completely. Work to get a full range of motion. Then pull yourself back up again and repeat. You may not be able to do three sets of ten with this exercise, but you should try to do three sets of as many pull-ups as you can do at the time. You'll be surprised how quickly you'll get better at them.

Pull-ups get the joint stretched out. You can hang on the bar a little bit and stretch out the ligaments and tendons for all the pushing exercises you've been doing. They also help to lengthen the muscle. The ideal muscle for throwing is long and flexible. Muscles that are not trained get tight and short. Weight lifting will enhance the tone of that muscle, make it long, and give it more elasticity.

a quarterback's workout

Another exercise that I do from a supine position is the **pull-over** (Figure 7.9). It's great for increasing the range of motion of the shoulder and for stretching out all the muscles of the shoulder. This is also an exercise that you do with very little weight.

Figure 7.9a

Figure 7.9b

Figure 7.9c

Figure 7.9d

Figure 7.9e

Figure 7.9f

Begin by lying on your back on a bench with your head extending out over the end. Take a light dumbbell in both hands, holding it toward one end, with your elbows bent slightly. With the weight hanging below the level of your head, pull it to a position over your upper chest, and then lower it back to its starting position. Take your time, using a pace of two counts up and four counts down, as described earlier. The important point here is to keep your elbows bent at the same angle throughout the entire range of motion. This will focus the effects of the exercise more effectively on the muscles supporting the shoulder joint rather than the elbow. Start off very lightly and gradually work your way up to a competitive weight, doing the full three sets of ten. Make sure you breathe properly while you do this exercise. Take a full breath, inhale deeply as you let the weight down, and exhale just as fully as you pull the weight back up again. That will also help expand the thoracic cavity and the chest muscles and will really give you a bigger, fuller range of motion.

Figure 7.10a

Figure 7.10b

External rotations (Figure 7.10), done as the last exercise in your workout, are great for tuning up the rotators and creating greater integrity at the shoulder joint. For this one you'll need a rolled-up towel, bench, and a light dumbbell—three to five pounds maximum. Begin by lying on your side on the bench. Place the rolled-up towel under your arm, in the armpit, so that it separates your upper arm from your side and supports it. The towel will position the shoulder joint so you can focus your work

a quarterback's workout

on just the right muscles. With all the different muscles that insert at the shoulder, you have to be careful to position the joint just right, so you can target the muscles you're after. Now take the small dumbbell in your hand so the palm is down and your elbow is bent at 90 degrees. The rolled-up towel should be under your arm, in the armpit. Your arm should be bent 90 degrees, and you should be holding a light dumbbell so that your palm is down (three to five pounds maximum for young athletes, ten to fifteen for a well-conditioned adult). Your elbow should be against your side. Now raise the dumbbell about 80 degrees, keeping your elbow at your side. Take your time and do three sets of ten, working very lightly. I've been doing this for years and I still don't work with any more than ten pounds. If you use heavier weights, you'll work only the large muscles and not these small ones that we're trying to target. So stay light. And, as before, bring the weight up on two counts and down on four.

Again, remember to do this exercise last, after you've done all the other shoulder exercises with both arms. We always try to work both sides of the body equally.

Don't try to do all of these exercises every time you work out. Pick a few—one or two from each category—and work out three times a week, so that when the week is over, you'll have done all the exercises no more than twice. For example, let's say on Monday you do three sets of bench presses, shoulder presses, pull-ups, and external rotations. That's a pretty heavy combination, but a good way start to start the week. On Wednesday you could lighten up the workout with pull-overs, inclined bench presses, and external rotations. Then, on Friday, you could toughen up the workout again with a full complement of dumbbell bench presses, shoulder presses, and pull-ups.

WEIGHT LIFTING MUSCLE CATEGORIES AND EXERCISES

Front Shoulder Muscles
Bench presses
Dumbbell bench presses
Pull-overs
Inclined bench presses

Back Shoulder Muscles
Bent-over lateral raises
Pull-ups

Middle Shoulder Muscles
Shoulder presses
Bent-over lateral raises

Rotator Cuff Muscles
External rotations

I'm being deliberately vague about the structure of these workouts because I don't want to push you into a routine that may not be appropriate for you. Weights and repetitions depend on your level of conditioning and your goals. The most important thing to remember in putting together any workout from these exercises is that you should use one exercise from each of the target muscle categories: one that affects the anterior muscles, one that affects the middle group of muscles, and one that affects the posterior muscle group.

I like to think of this workout as a year-round program. During the off-season, it's a good idea to go three times a week and really push yourself. You want to work harder with heavier weights and try to build strength and endurance. During the playing season, you should cut back. Go twice a week and work fairly lightly—at least 10 to 20 percent lighter than your normal off-season workout. The purpose in this is to maintain the strength you've built in the off-season.

a quarterback's workout

CHAPTER 8
Game Day

Figure 8.0   Leadership. Ten grown men and all eyes are staring at me; they're listening and believing everything I say. It just shows you the power you have as the quarterback. It's important that coaches teach the quarterback to know how much power he has and to use it in the best interests of his team to reach their goals.

SKILLS PLUS EXPERIENCE

NFL quarterbacks have to be much more skilled today. I think that's probably why you don't see many young quarterbacks doing that well as they enter the league. It takes a lot of time for many of them. Even the best will take a few years to get to the point where they really understand what they're doing and what to expect from their receivers. The receivers also need time to work on the skills and timing needed to fit with each quarterback's delivery.

—Mark Bavaro
Tight End, New York Giants
1985–1990

There comes a time, once a week during the fall and early winter, when it's time to measure what you've accomplished during the off-season and training camp. Whether it's Friday night or Saturday or Sunday afternoon...or even Monday night, it's still called game day. Everyone prepares for it in his own way. A lot of players like to do the same thing, the same way, every time as they get ready to play. They eat the same food. They wear the same things. All their preparations are the same. It puts their mind at ease and helps them to play better.

I never really had a regular pregame routine. I didn't eat much on game day, but that's about all I could say was consistent for me. Early in my career I guess you could say I went through a quiet stage, when I was calm and worked at being quiet and focused. I'd study a little more. But in my later years I was just the opposite.

game day

Figure 8.1   Getting ready, Chicago, 1993. Dave Brown, Kent Graham, and I are getting ready for the first game of the season against the Bears. I'm loose and they're
probably sick of the same old stories.

I walked around the locker room and talked to the other guys and got ready to have a good time. One of the coaches would yell that we had five minutes to go, and I'd go put on my shoulder pads. I had studied all week and practiced hard. There was no need to cram. It was time for everything to happen naturally. For me, I guess the relaxed approach was best. My mind was clear, and I was loose and just ready to play (Figure 8.1).

Much of your success on any given day will depend on how well you know the opposing team and its potential weaknesses. Of course, the key is recognizing those vulnerabilities when you see them and having the presence of mind and tools available to exploit them. Your coaches will prepare you as a team.

But on a personal level, your individual performance will depend on a few individual skills like concentration and your ability to see what's going on around you. It will depend on the confidence you have in your abilities and ultimately, of course, with your skill as a passer. If your primary receiver is covered and your secondary is open in the flat, will you see him in time and will you get the ball to him consistently, under heavy pressure, so that he can catch it? Can you stand under center and look over the defense in a glance and anticipate which of your receivers has the greatest potential of getting open, given the defensive set and the patterns you've called? These questions and many more like them are what game day is all about.

LIMITING YOUR CHOICES

Finding the open receiver under game conditions is a challenge at any level of the game but it's particularly rough on young, junior quarterbacks who are just learning the position. The tendency is either to focus on one receiver and watch him all the way through

game day

EXPECTATIONS

The quarterback should expect each receiver involved in a given play to understand the whole play—all the patterns. If you're the tight end, you have to understand the complementary routes that are being run by the wide receivers and the running backs. You've got to know where all the receivers are on the field and where your pattern fits into the whole play. Each receiver has boundaries in any given play and he's got to know where he can go and where he can't go. He's got to know how many steps the quarterback is dropping, if it's a three-, five-, or seven-step drop. He's got to know how much time he has to get out there. And he's got to know the coverage.

—Mark Bavaro
Tight End, New York Giants
1985–1990

his pattern or to try to look at too many receivers in too many different directions. The key at all levels is to limit your choices as early as possible and to set up priorities and alternatives that are reasonably simple to execute. At the higher levels the decision process also includes reading the defensive coverage.

I'm not going to go into great detail about reading defenses and individual coverage because it's so complex I could write another book about it. But I will tell you that you can easily limit your choices and increase the odds that you'll complete a high percentage of your passes if you follow a very simple decision process.

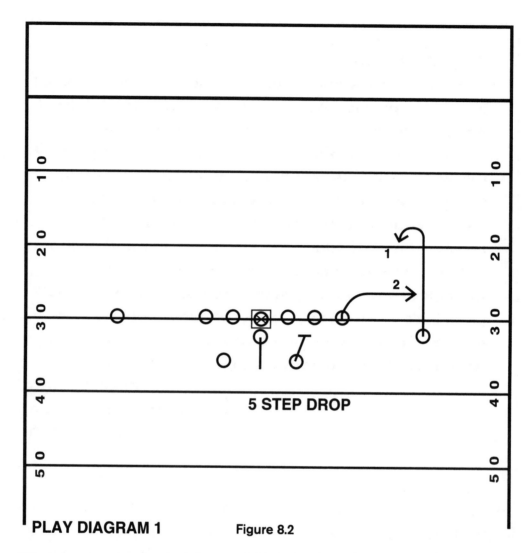

PLAY DIAGRAM 1   Figure 8.2

There are so many levels of football, starting with Pee Wee, high school, college, and the pros. Obviously, as the level increases, so does the sophistication of the passing game.

In the beginning I would make the decision process as simple as possible. Come to the line of scrimmage, and look over the defense as you take your position under center, thinking about the play that's called and about the routes your receivers are supposed to take, visualizing them in advance if you can. Let's say, for

PLAY DIAGRAM 2　　　　　Figure 8.3

example, that you have two receivers going out: one outside on the right, running a ten-yard curl or hook pattern, and another receiver going out five yards to the right flat (Figure 8.2). Begin by taking a five-step drop and looking to the deep pattern first—the ten-yard curl.

If he's open, throw the football. If not, hold on to it and smoothly re-shift your weight, turn, and look for the five-yard out. Again, if he's open, throw it. If not, throw the ball over the receiver's head or run the football if the run is open. There's nothing very complex here. At the younger level, that's really all you should be doing—thinking first guy, second guy, throw it away. Never hesitate. That's the decision process: **one, two, throw it away**.

In high school I would take the process one step further. Taking the same play with a ten-yard curl and a five-yard out, a coach would probably add a third receiver as an outlet (Figure 8.3). This is somebody who might go through the middle of the line, set a block, and end up three or four yards ahaed of you or a little to one side.

In this situation I wouldn't say that you have three receivers; I would say that you have two, and if neither one is open, you can dump the ball to the outlet receiver. The decision process this time is **one, two, dump it**.

Think about it. Picture yourself at the line. You're under center, looking over the defense, thinking about the patterns you have called. Only this time, you're thinking **one, two, dump it**. Make your five-step drop and look at the ten-yard curl. If it's not there, look for the five-yard out. If it's covered, dump it to the outlet, if he's open. If he's covered, throw it into the ground short of the receiver's feet. Remember, no hesitation: **one, two, dump it**.

Remember it and do it that way every time. In practice, when you go through your patterns and you hit each receiver in the play, you should execute the whole decision process as you would under game conditions. The first time through, hit the primary receiver (the ten-yard curl). Then, on the second run, look primary, re-shift, and hit the secondary pattern (the five-yard flat). On the next try, throw the dump. But don't just take the snap, drop, and throw the

PLAY DIAGRAM 3   Figure 8.4

DUMP

5 STEP DROP

game day

dump. Drop and look for the first receiver, then the second, and then look for the dump and throw it: **one, two, dump it**. Practice the patterns the way you expect to throw them for real, because that's the timing sequence you will experience in the game. Get used to it that way: **one, two, dump it**.

At the college level, the patterns can get a little more complicated. For instance, you might add a third pattern and then a dump (Figure 8.4). So, the passing decision would be **one, two, three,**

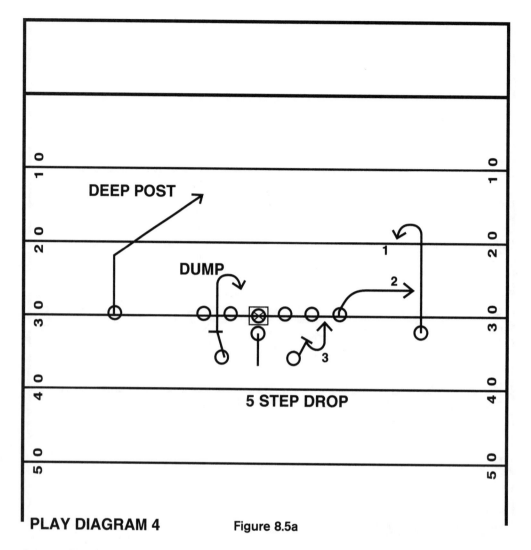

PLAY DIAGRAM 4   Figure 8.5a

dump it. Again, no hesitation: Look at receiver number one. If the pass isn't there, look for two. If you can't throw to number two, go to three. If three is covered, dump the ball. Again, if the dump man isn't open, throw the ball into the ground short of the receiver's feet. That's really the only big difference in the decision process as you advance from one level to the next in the nonprofessional ranks.

In the pros you'll have to read the coverage. Again, we'll keep it simple. Let's say you've got a similar play called; on the right side, you've

DEEP POST

S

DUMP

5 STEP DROP

PLAY DIAGRAM 4A Figure 8.5b

got a ten-yard curl, a five-yard out and a pattern we called a "check-m" coming out of the backfield and a dump route somewhere near the middle, just over the line. The only difference in the pros is that on the other side you might have a receiver running a deep post (Figure 8.5a). So as you stand under center and look out over the defense, this time you might say to yourself, if the safety moves out of the middle to help out on the right, I'll look for the deep post first (Figure 8.5b). But, let's say you take your first step off the line and the safety stays where he is. In that case you stick with the timing patterns you called on the right. Just before you land on your fifth step, look for one. If he's covered, look for two and then dump it if you don't find anyone open. If the safety moves out of the middle as you drop, look for the deep post first—if he is there as you land, throw it. If he isn't, then go straight to the dump. Do *not* go to the receivers on the right. Remember, the other three routes you've got called are timing routes. If you try to go for the long route and it isn't there, it's too late to go back to the other patterns. You've lost the timing.

One more point here. Coaches should teach their quarterbacks to take their first couple of steps looking straight up the field, to avoid any hint of where he's planning to throw the football.

Wait until you're just about ready to take your last step of the drop before you turn and look at your first receiver. You'll need that little bit of time to focus on the area where you intend to throw. If you turn and look for your pattern right away, you'll tell the defense exactly where you're going. Moreover, it will upset your timing. You'll have the tendency to want to throw the football before the pass is ready to happen. Look upfield so that you can maintain the rhythm of the drop and it coincides with the timing of the pattern. If you turn and look to your receiver right away, you'll lose some of the rhythm and spontaneity that you need to throw the ball on time. You'll want to throw it too soon. On timing routes you should know where the receiver is going to be. You've practiced it a thousand times. Don't look for him too early. When you land, he'll either be there or he won't. Pass or go on. Never hesitate.

NO WAITING

When you drop back, one of the worst things is to have to wait before you can throw the football. As you stand there, waiting for

THROWING IN THE NFL TODAY: There's not a lot of time to waste. Today, in the pros, you have to have the ability to throw the ball with both velocity and accuracy because there's not a lot of reaction time available when you drop to throw. The ball can't be in the air for long because of the speed of the defenders these days. They're so quick that when a receiver does make a move, it's not like he's open very long. So you have to be able to throw with velocity when you need it, and, of course, you have to be accurate. You also need to be a good decision maker, and you have to be confident. You've got to make your decision and not second-guess yourself. Don't hesitate. You're not going to make the right decision all the time. I've always been a guy who likes to drop back, decide what I'm going to do, and then turn it loose and throw the football—just make my decision and do it.

–Dan Marino
Quarterback, Miami Dolphins

game day

someone to break loose, the tendency is to tighten up. You start to lose the natural rhythm of passing, and the odds are that you'll throw some bad footballs. Coaches have really just started teaching this technique over the past few years, but it's pretty widely accepted. As you watch quarterbacks throw at all levels, you'll see that their timing has improved considerably. More quarterbacks throw with better rhythm. There's no hesitation. They don't have to stand and wait. They don't have to hop around, and they don't build up tension in their bodies. So they stay relaxed and perform at a higher level.

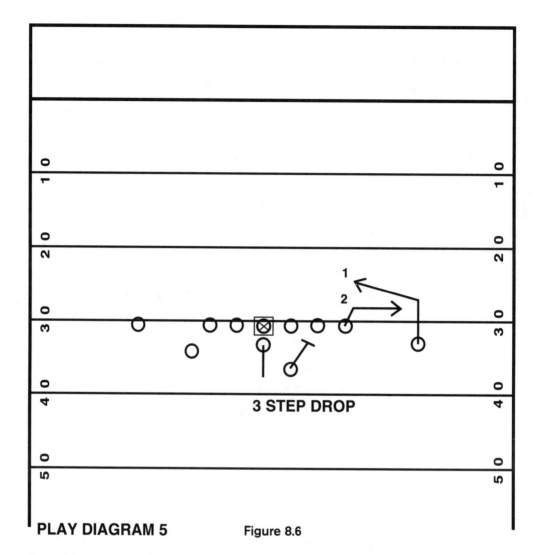

3 STEP DROP

PLAY DIAGRAM 5   Figure 8.6

Another quick point: In the play we've been scheming, you've got a ten-to-twelve yard curl called on the right side. Why do we say ten to twelve yards? Why the variation? Remember, these are timing routes. If the receiver slips or gets bumped off the line, he's got to cut his pattern short so he can get to the final position on time. If he gets a clean release and nobody is in the way, he can run the pattern to twelve. The receiver has to have that feel as things happen in the game, so he can time-up with the quarterback.

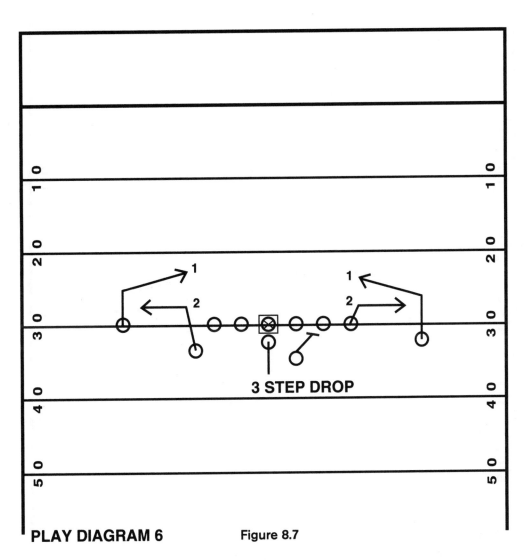

PLAY DIAGRAM 6   Figure 8.7

THREE STEPS

When you run a pass off a three-step drop, the decision process for a young player should not go any further than **one, two:** first receiver, second receiver (Figure 8.6). Realistically, there's no time for anything else. The defensive linemen know it's a three-step drop.

If you take any more time than one, two, three, land, and throw, you're going to get buried, or the ball is going to get tipped. So just before that third step hits, look at the first receiver. If he's

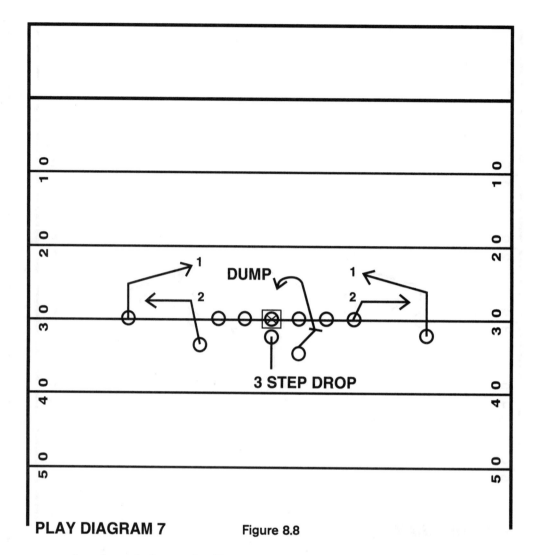

PLAY DIAGRAM 7   Figure 8.8

open, land and throw it. If not, re-gather yourself and go directly to number two. Again, coaches at this level should limit a play like this to one side or the other.

At the high school level, since you'll probably have the same routes called on both sides (Figure 8.7), you should come up and look at the defense and determine which side has fewer defenders. If the defense is shifted strong to your right, then get ready to throw left. If it's rotated to your left, then prepare to throw right. If everything is equal—if the defense is balanced equally on both sides—look for your best receiver first, or throw to the side where you throw best. At a young age you should throw in the direction you throw best. When you get older and you're more consistent as a passer, throw it to the guy who can do more with the ball: Jerry Rice, for example.

Coaches at the higher levels will often add a dump pattern to this play (Figure 8.8). They will scheme the remaining back to check and release over the middle three or four yards as an outlet pattern. So this time, when the quarterback lands, he looks for one. If he's not there, he looks for two. If he's covered, he turns and dumps immediately. What do you do if the dump isn't there? Throw the ball into the ground. There's no time for anything else. The decision has to be that quick with no hesitation. This is really more of a pro scheme. College coaches would probably stick with choosing one side or the other and then throwing to the open receiver on that side. But that really depends on the coach and the skills of the individual quarterback.

SEVEN STEPS

Seven-step drops give you a little more time and the opportunity to scheme some deeper patterns. You can run play-action passes, too, but we're not going to cover those here. We'll stick with straight drop-back passing.

Let's say, for example, that you have a play set up that calls for your outside receivers on both sides to run ten-yard outs and then turn up the field (Figure 8.9). They're going deep. They play also calls for two shallow patterns: five-yard outs to both flats. What do you do? Like the three-step drop, you first look at the

game day

RHYTHM

The quarterback has to know his receivers—the way they move, the way they catch the ball, how fast they are. And the receivers need to know the quarterback—the way he throws the ball, the time it takes him to run his drops, the touch he has on the ball. And that takes a lot of practice and game experience. You get two new guys (a new quarterback and a receiver) working together and the rhythm is not going to be there right away. And passing the football is a rhythm game. It's like a dance. The quarterback is going to take his steps and the receiver has to take his so that it all comes together with everyone in the right place at the right time when the opportunity comes to throw the football. If either one of them is off step or off speed, the whole play can fall apart. Over time, the partners gain confidence in each other. The more confidence they develop, the smoother the dance. The more the quarterback finds his receiver in the right place at the right time, the more he's going to throw the ball to him. Ideally, he's got to develop that relationship with all his receivers.

If the quarterback loses confidence in one or more of them, it can throw his whole game off as he starts second-guessing where he can throw the ball. If he sees the back of his receiver's helmet moving down the field, twenty or thirty yards away, the question becomes, is he going to throw it? Does he have enough faith in that guy to know that he will turn around at the right time to catch the ball? A lot of times, the ball has to be thrown before the receiver is looking. And, it takes an awful lot of faith for a quarterback to lay it out there like that, hoping that the receiver will make the right moves and turn around when he's supposed to so that *he* catches the football and not the defensive back.

When a receiver runs a seam straight up the field, many times, a quarterback can't see him. He can't really see if he's open or not because there's usually a defensive back trailing him. And he doesn't often know what the distance is between them. So when he lays the ball up there, he has to rely on a certain amount of faith that the receiver is running the right way and that he's going to look at the right time.

Phil used to do that a lot when I'd run the seam. I wasn't always open but he always threw it, even though he might not have seen exactly where I was going. But he knew in a way. He had confidence because we'd done it so many times before. When I played with other quarterbacks after I left the Giants, it took time to develop that kind of confidence between us.

So, there is a relationship that develops between receivers and quarterbacks in a team system over time. Look at Jerry Rice in San Francisco. He's a phenomenal athlete. You can't say a bad word about him. He's just unbelievable. Add to that the fact that he's been in the same system, running the same patterns with the same quarterbacks (Montana, Bono, and Young) his whole career and you can see why he's been so successful. Steve Young was always there as a backup before he took over the lead role.

It's just like when Jeff Hostetler stepped in for Phil in 1990. Things didn't really miss a beat too much. They changed but they stayed pretty even-keeled because we all knew Jeff. We had all practiced with him and had a relationship with him.

Compare Jerry Rice with Andre Risen, who is also a phenomenal athlete, catching all those balls down in Atlanta. Then he gets picked up and moves to Cleveland, and look at his numbers in his first year. They're not there because he doesn't have the same relationship yet. That's not to say he won't ever get it. It's just going to take time and patience to develop.

–Mark Bavaro
Tight End, New York Giants
1985–1990

game day

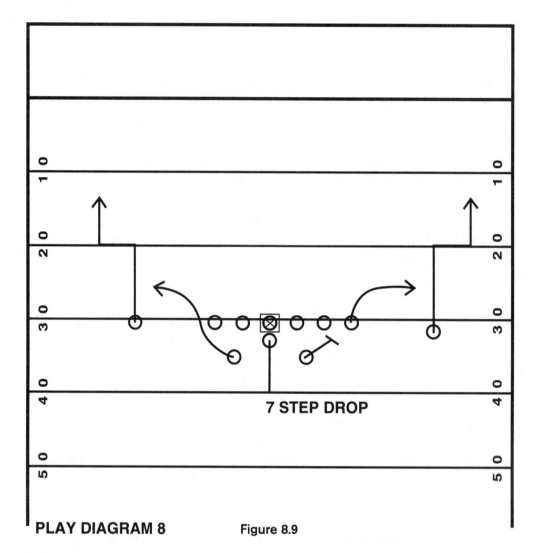

PLAY DIAGRAM 8   Figure 8.9

defense for any shift to strength and consider throwing away from it. If the defense is balanced, then pick a side that favors your best receiver, the weaker defender, or whatever advantage you might think you have at the time, prior to the snap.

Your receivers can also run maneuver routes off of a seven-step drop. Because they know the quarterback is taking seven steps, they can make more than one move or run double routes (Figure 8.10). For example, one receiver could run ten to twelve yards up, fake a

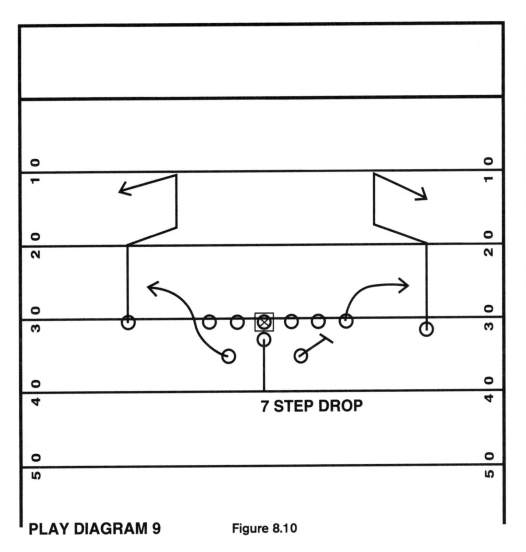

PLAY DIAGRAM 9   Figure 8.10

step to the outside, turn back up the field, and then plant and come back at anywhere from eighteen to twenty yards.

The coach may very well run the same thing on the other side: Ten yards up, fake the out, turn up for ten more, plant, and come back to eighteen. That's the ideal situation: Plant at twenty and catch the ball at eighteen. So what do you tell the quarterback? We've already talked about all the basic techniques.

game day

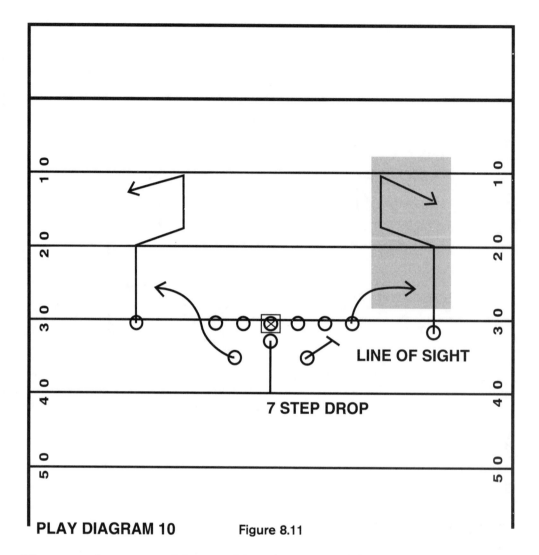

PLAY DIAGRAM 10   Figure 8.11

The most important thing to do at the snap of the ball is to get depth. Turn around and get off the line fast and take your seven steps. Stay under control, but get back there so you can look out over the field and get yourself set. You need time to get everything in order, to see the whole field and take your slide-and-gather step to add forward momentum to your throw. Remember, you're throwing the ball a good distance down the field and to the outside. So, you need all the power you can muster.

TIMING

The receiver expects the quarterback to get him the ball the moment he's open. He's working hard to break loose. When he turns around he expects the quarterback to have the ball in the air coming at him or for him to be looking in his direction about to throw the ball. You're only open for split seconds in football, for the most part. You don't ever want to be hanging out there waiting for the ball to get to you. That's when people start coming at you. And that's when you get laid out. Receivers want the ball coming split seconds after they turn their heads. That gives the defensive backs and linebackers as little time as possible to react. Quarterbacks and receivers both need that. Football is definitely a game of timing.

–Mark Bavaro
Tight End, New York Giants
1985–1990

game day

What do you do if your maneuver routes are covered? You can throw to the shallow pattern. First of all, this is probably more advanced than you want to get for younger players. The patterns are too long, and the secondary routes are more difficult to pick up. And even with the depth you get from seven steps, the line would have trouble maintaining their blocks. I'd say the earliest you'd want to run this type of scheme would be in high school.

ONE LINE OF SIGHT

Limiting your search to one side is the easiest way to find both your deep and shallow receivers when you're running double maneuver

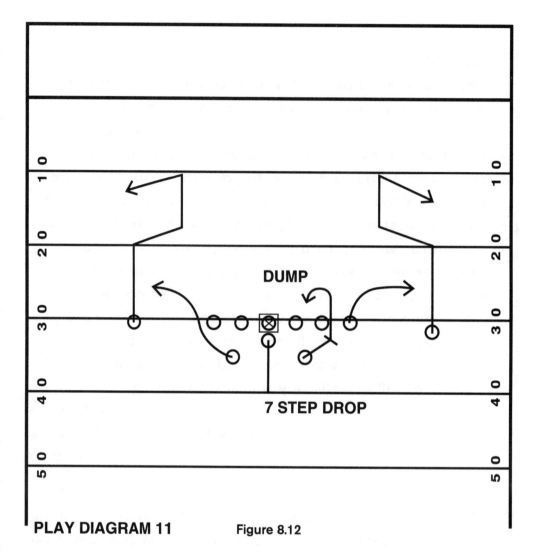

PLAY DIAGRAM 11   Figure 8.12

routes with shallow patterns underneath (Figure 8.11). Both your receivers should be in the same line of sight. You always want to keep them where you can see both routes with minimal effort. Never ask a quarterback at any level to look for one receiver on one side of the field and then turn to find another on the opposite side. It's just not going to happen, at least not very often.

So, using this approach, you've got two decisions to make; left side vs. right side, and deep vs. shallow. Your first decision is at

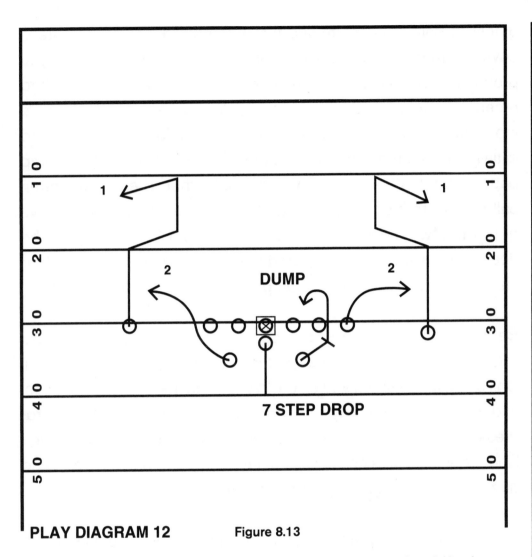

PLAY DIAGRAM 12   Figure 8.13

the line of scrimmage. Look to see if the defense is shifted one way or the other. If they're strong to one side, think about throwing to the opposite side. You want to throw away from the strength of the defense.

Once you've decided right or left, your next read comes just before you land on your last step of the seven-step drop. Keep your toes to the sideline and your front shoulder pointed downfield, and read the deep receiver first. If he's open, slide and

game day

gather to gain momentum and throw the ball. If the deep route is covered, then go to the short route on the same side. As you progress, you can add a dump pattern. He can be your third receiver (Figure 8.12). Coaches usually scheme this receiver to move across the line a few yards over the middle. If he's covered initially, he can move a little to either side to get free. Your dump pattern shouldn't be in a hurry to get out either. The play will often call for him to hit a defender as he goes out. Remember, you've got a **one, two** decision to make first (Figure 8.13): looking for the deep maneuver route or the short flat *on the same side*. Your third choice for either side is the dump. Again, it's **one, two, dump it**.

Be sure to practice the sequence of patterns the way you would execute them in a game situation: look long, throw long; look long, look short, throw short; and so on. Work at mastering the techniques, and learn to throw in rhythm. Drop back and go through the progression. It should feel smooth as you complete the steps. As you land on your last step, it should feel like hit...one...two...and dump. It's all rhythm. Never break the rhythm.

Even when you get pressure, your thought process should stay the same—relaxed and under control. If you're under severe pressure, sometimes you've got to go one, two...throw it away. You can't even look for the dump. Sometimes you have to throw it away after the first guy. You won't even get to two. Experience will teach you to read the pressure and the other elements around you. There's no doubt in my mind that if I've got an untouched defender barreling in on me and my number one receiver is covered and there's no time to look for two, I'm throwing it away, right now.

READ AND READ AGAIN: Regardless of all the pre-reads that you get, your blitz pickups and all, you still have to read the defense after you get the ball and you start your drop back to decide where to throw it. You'll get a pretty good idea where you're going to be able to throw. A lot of the time, you can preread...you can say to yourself while you're standing up there that this is going to be the guy I'm going to throw to and you're going to be absolutely right. And there will be other times when that's not going to be the case. So you also have to read it after the snap. Read the coverage and make your decision. You really have to look at the whole picture. Most of the time safeties will give you a real good idea what the coverage is. And then there are also the outside techniques or inside techniques of the defenders that will help determine the coverage on a particular side. Based on how the defenders are playing, you're going to have a real good idea where you can go with the football. Then it really comes down to whether your receiver can win if it's a one-on-one situation: that is, win versus the technique that's being played against him. Of course, then it's your job to get the ball to where he can catch it.

—Dan Marino
Quarterback, Miami Dolphins

game day

MOVING IN THE POCKET

Learning to move in the pocket begins with doing the drills we described in Chapter 3. The **pocket drill** teaches you to stay calm and relaxed when you drop back, to move a step at a time, always under control, always in the position to throw, ball in both hands, with your front shoulder pointed downfield and your toes to the sideline. In addition to that, what we did in the pros was work with line outside of group offense, to develop our timing in the pocket. I've seen some high school programs do it, too. When the offensive line was going through their pass-blocking drills, learning the fronts for that week, I would go and stand behind them and mentally go through my reads and get a feel for where I should be under pressure and learn to maneuver and not alter my thought process as I moved. So, if I'm taking a five-step drop, and I want to throw to the outside receiver, if he's not there, then I have to step up almost automatically without thinking. Where do I go now? I react on a physical level. The pressure is here, so I auto-matically step up or over, all the while keeping my rhythm: one . . . two . . . dump. You can't rush it. You'll know that you're start-ing to turn into a pretty good quarterback when you land on the last step of your drop and you always have a nice relaxed attitude and thought process. Regardless of how frenzied everything is around you, you're not panicked or tunnel-visioned. You're under control, and you can see clearly and the rhythm is right there. A good habit to get into when you go up to the line to set up under center is to take a deep breath and just let it go. Blow out some air and just relax. The more relaxed you are, the better you will throw the ball and the clearer your decision making will be. If you go up there all hyped up and tight, you'll probably rush everything, including your passing mechanics and decision process, increas-ing the potential for error.

Early in my career, I had to stand in the pocket sometimes for longer than I wanted, looking for a receiver, and I paid the price several times. But that was a different era in football. The game

The passing game has changed because the defensive players are becoming faster and faster. So the quarterback's mechanics have to be almost perfect. It's like a fighter, a professional boxer. Unless his fundamentals are good, he will never make it. So he spars in the gym by the hour with a guy right next to him telling him what to do: block left hook, block right hand, counterpunch, all these things. And he has to become so good at seeing and anticipating those things that he obviously doesn't think about it in the ring. Well, those kinds of skills have to be developed in a quarterback because it's just as harrowing for him to have these defensive guys unloading on him. And if his mechanics aren't ultra-perfect, as good as they can get, then he's going to take more punishment, and his effectiveness will drop way off. And that's where we are now in the NFL. How much of that is emphasized, and how many people are alert to it? Not that many.

—Bill Walsh
Retired Head Coach, Stanford University
Former Head Coach, San Francisco 49ers

game day

wasn't as clear-cut and as well defined as it is now. The job description for the position is much more disciplined today than it was fifteen years ago or even ten years ago. There's a big difference between now and ten years ago at all levels. Now you're asked to perform at a much higher level, and the game is more refined. The timing is more precise. When I first started playing, we had maybe one timing pattern—a ten-yard out. That was about it. The rest of the passing game called for the quarterback to stand in the pocket and wait, to stay there as long as you could and throw the ball when somebody got open. The goal was quick yardage. Shorter timing patterns just weren't that much of the game at the time. A few coaches were using them—Bill Walsh at San Francisco, for example, but very few others.

Today, I wouldn't teach a quarterback to do what I did then. I wouldn't coach him to stand back there in the pocket until the last possible second, because if it doesn't happen in the prescribed time as you've learned and practiced it, ninety-nine times out of a hundred it's not going to happen. Okay, maybe nineteen out of twenty times. In either case, standing there waiting and waiting is a dangerous waste of time. If the pass isn't open within the pre-scribed time, it's probably not going to happen. Sure, you can scramble and make a play here and there (Figure 8.14), but in the long run you'll make more mistakes than positive yardage.

There are some pro quarterbacks who made great plays getting out of the pocket and scrambling to get some phenomenal pass off. You see them on the weekly highlight reels all the time. But if you were to do a little research and break down the passing per-centages, if you looked at a comparison of their success inside the pocket as opposed to outside, you would see that it is vastly counterproductive when they break out of the pocket. You'd look at the numbers and swear it isn't true. But it's been done. I've seen the studies. For some of them, their percentages drop to a fraction of their normal drop-back percentages. Our perception is that quarterbacks make great plays when they're out there; but there's a reason why some of them have been sacked over a hun-dred times in one year. They get sacked because they break the

Figure 8.14   Good mechanics. Even though I'm getting hit, my weight is shifted over my left foot and the ball is off. My right foot is off the ground. My left knee is slightly bent and my foot is planted and pointed toward my target as it should be. My hips are finishing their rotation in spite of the tackler.

game day

timing of a play trying to create situations. It's exciting when it happens, and sometimes it can win ball games, but in the long run the numbers show that a steady diet of it is detrimental.

Football is a team sport. To my mind it's the greatest team sport invented. When you have timing patterns called, your receivers are running routes that are supposed to time up with your drop. So what is the line doing? Well, they know how long it should take to throw from a five-step drop. They know when the pass should be gone. If it's not, if the quarterback is holding on to the ball too long, there's a good chance he's going to get sacked. When you've practiced the timing of the play over and over, the guys on the line know that should have been enough time. So what happened? You held on to the ball too long, waiting for something to happen, and the play broke down somewhere. It all has to work together. The line is an integral part of the timing aspect of the passing game.

They know what the timing is for each play. On the seven-step drop, they know that's a long time. Each one of them understands that he has to work and keep on working because the quarterback's back there deep. He knows he's got little more ground to give but it's going to take the quarterback longer to throw the ball, because the receivers are running longer and more complex routes.

When the pressure is on, and the defense is closing in, number one, you want to try to stay in the pocket. That's where the line has set up to protect you. Unless you have a serious breakdown in the middle, most of the pressure is going to come from the outside. So your best move most of the time is going to be a step up, into the pocket, toward the center. They key is not to panic. We've studied the steps. You've seen the drill in Chapter 3. Step and glide, a step at a time,

Figure 8.15 It's difficult to complete a good follow-through when your throwing hand is pinned to your face mask. Obviously, I didn't get a lookout block on this pass attempt.

under control, looking for your receivers to break open; thinking to yourself as you look, one...two...dump...or throw or whatever is appropriate. It all fits together. You learn to put it all together with time and practice and experience. You work on the pocket drill. You do it in practice. And when you look at the game film or tape you see what happens when you do it right, and you see sometimes that if you had stepped up the way you've practiced and drilled you could have done better. Eventually you learn to look downfield and see space around you and step accordingly.

game day

189

Figure 8.16 You've got to stay focused and fundamentally sound, especially when you're under pressure.

TAKING THE HIT

If you are throwing properly, you're nice and relaxed and loose. So there are going to be many times, at all levels, that you can see or sense that somebody is going to hit you, but you still have to throw the ball (Figure 8.15). If you stay relaxed, you have a better chance of throwing the ball well; if you're relaxed when they hit you, you will absorb the blow much better. The same is true as you fall and hit the turf. You don't want to tighten up and try to stop the impact. You very seldom get hit without knowing it's coming. The blind-side hit happens to everybody, but not that much—maybe a couple of times a year. And the higher the level, the fewer of them you can absorb. Of course, if you're relaxed when you throw, you're going to be relaxed when you get hit.

There were several times when we ran what Dan Reeves called scramble passes: scramble left and scramble right. You drop back as though you're doing a straight drop-back, and as you hit that last step, you run to the outside, toward the sideline, left or right, whichever way the scramble is called. Then you set up and throw the ball down the field (Figure 8.16). I did a couple of those early in my career, and I can remember rolling out and hearing my lineman yelling "Look out! Look out, Phil!" And I would throw the ball real quick and sort of duck and relax and someone would go flying right over the top of me. It would have been a blind-side disaster, but because the play took so much time to develop, the move was so long, and I had to hold on to the ball for such a long time, I was able to get a "look out" block.

Some defender is bound to get free, but if he's aware enough, a lineman has time to yell, and you can usually hear it. I've also had a couple of situations where I was running a scramble pass, getting ready to throw the football, and I swear I heard the crowd go, "Wooo..." making that ominous groan they make when something bad is going to happen. And I would throw the ball, but having felt impact all too many times right after hearing that groan, I knew I was about to get clobbered by somebody who was getting free behind me. And the crowd had alerted me. So I got rid of the ball quick and dropped. And my instincts were right. Somebody was just about to bury me.

game day

> **THROWING IN POOR WEATHER**
> It's important to have mental toughnes to deal with the changing weather conditions that a quarterback faces from day to day in Buffalo. When you are facing forty- to fifty-mile-per-hour winds on the field, it is important that you have good mechanics and follow through on all your passes. You cannot depend on arm strength alone.
>
> —Jim Kelly
> Quarterback, Buffalo Bills

A good example of where that didn't happen was the 1990–1991 N.F.C. championship game when Joe Montana scrambled right and Leonard Marshall hit him from behind. Joe got knocked out of the game and broke a finger or something. But the reason given by the 49ers bench for his absence for the rest of the game was overall body ache. That really summed it up. Joe wasn't fortunate enough to get a "look out" block or a reaction from the crowd to alert him to what was coming. But I was lucky enough to avoid a few of those bone-rattling hits just because of crowd noise and "look out" blocks.

PLAYING IN BAD WEATHER
Wind

I developed a certain way to throw in the wind. And I think it was only because I had to do it so much through practice and game conditions at Giants Stadium that I just taught myself a different way to throw when it was windy.

My number one criterion when it was windy was to throw a spiral. I taught myself some unique ways to do that: I dropped my shoulder; I cupped the ball little more; I did all these things that helped to control the ball and create rotation so I could get it through the wind. I didn't know enough about my fundamental techniques at that time. So out of necessity I developed certain techniques so I could throw in spite of the elements. They worked for me, but they're not something you'd want to teach anyone else. In fact, when Jim Fassel was a quarterback coach with Denver, it was pretty windy one day, and he was telling his quarterbacks about how I could throw spirals in the wind. He showed them what I did.

They went out to warm up before practice, and Jim saw John Elway, one of the best passers ever, trying to do all these things that I did to try and get the ball through the wind, and he was having a heck of a time because it was so awkward for him. And it should have been. So you really couldn't teach it. That was my adjustment. I really didn't know completely how I did it. I just developed these bad techniques over time. But it was only because I had nothing else to fall back on. I just learned to have that certain feel when I needed to so that I could keep the ball spinning the way it needed to in the wind.

If I could start over now, coming to the Giants as a quarterback who is smarter about throwing the football, I would never make those adjustments. Number one, I'd be a little more conservative in my decision making. If it's a beautiful day and you've got a receiver downfield, you can take the chance and try to stick the ball in there sometimes. You can go for the longer gain. But if it's windy, you can't take that chance. You've got to go for the shorter route instead.

game day

More important, I'd make sure my mechanics were sound. That would be my primary tool against the wind: good fundamental technique. You can't rush it either. The temptation at first is to speed up the throwing motion, to get more power. If anything, the opposite is true. Slow down the motion. Think about it: When you speed up and try to power the ball, what happens? You give up a certain amount of control. Most of the time you're going to lose part of the throwing sequence. And when you lose that sequence, anything can happen. Your accuracy definitely suffers. Now add the wind factor and you magnify those errors considerably more.

If you manipulate the ball even a little bit to make up for some fundamental mistake and get a little wobble on the ball, what happens? Within ten yards, it's gone. The ball is up for grabs. The only thing you can hope for is that so many guys will be fighting for it that someone will knock it down. Again, to use golf as a comparison, what do golfers do when they're hitting the ball into the wind? They swing slower, try to keep the ball down and put less force on it so it doesn't fly up into the wind. A lot of the same techniques apply to passing. Don't explode into the ball. You want to be nice and smooth, with average force. You will get through the wind, believe it or not, better than if you try to muscle it.

A great example: I watched the Raiders and the Giants practice on a Saturday, getting ready to play at Giants Stadium the following afternoon. The wind was blowing at least thirty to thirty-five miles per hour. I watched Vince Evans, who can spin the ball about as hard as anyone I've seen in the league. And he's out there, throwing into the wind, just rifling that ball to the target. About half of them were pretty decent throws. They'd get through the wind, and the receiver had a pretty good chance to make the catch. The rest of the time they'd just get away from him. And as he stood out there and kept throwing, suddenly he started just relaxing and putting the ball out there a lot softer and he had much better control. He figured it out. He learned a lesson there in about thirty minutes. You can't fight it. He learned to relax; he got more comfortable; he had better follow-through—all those things. It made a tremendous difference. You can't speed up the process or throw harder and expect to control the football. Think about what's going on: The motion itself has to be shorter because instinctively you grip the ball tighter, you tighten up the arm and shoulder muscles.

And all of that stops the natural, flowing motion and follow-through that really gives the ball rotation. When you tighten up, you actually lose a little spin, and that makes the ball less stable in the air. So the wind can take it wherever it wants

Rain

When it's raining, most of the professional quarterbacks are going up there thinking, "Oh man, I hope I get a grip." As you're dropping back, you're asking yourself, "Do I have a good grip or not? Does it feel good?" But the truth is, you don't have to change much of anything in the rain. You don't have to throw differently. Just try to be more accurate.

Why do some people have trouble throwing the ball when it's wet? Jim Fassel says that they squeeze the ball too hard. When you squeeze it too hard, when it's wet, he says it's going to squirt out for your hand. And you'll never be able to finish the throwing motion. Generally the rule of thumb is, if the ball is wet, you surely do not want to grip it tighter. If anything, maybe you'd grip it the same as you would normally, or a hair lighter. Don't tighten your grip.

game day

TOUGHNESS: In my last year in professional football, I was cut by the Giants and claimed by Phoenix. And guys like Freddy Joe Nunn and other good defensive players there, who had played against Simms, asked me about him right away. They were curious about what he was made of because they had a tremendous amount of respect for him. They said that some quarterbacks in the league, when you get to them early and often and really pound them, will fold their tent for the rest of the afternoon. But they said that Simms was a guy you could slam to the turf for fifty-eight minutes straight and he'd still find a way to get up off the ground in the last two minutes and beat you. He had a toughness that went beyond the physical: the kind of mental toughness that inspired the other players around him.

–Phil McConkey
Receiver, New York Giants
1984–1987

The other thing you should try is slowing down the whole sequence of throwing, 5 percent of normal; just enough to cut down the potential for error. Focus a little more on technique so you will have a better chance of controlling the ball.

LEADERSHIP

What is being a leader or having leadership qualities? Somebody said to me the other day, talking about a young quarterback, that it's hard for a young quarterback to be a leader for a lot of reasons.

Number one: People are only going to look up to you once you've accomplished something. You've got to do something first. That's the first thing that has to happen at any level. Go out there and do something well. And once you've had that success, people will look at you and might tend to believe more in what you're saying. I guess it could be analogous to two guys running businesses. Let's say that you have a company and I'm starting a company. You call me and try to tell me how to run my company. But your company is losing money, so I don't care about what you have to say. Why should I listen to you? You have no credibility. The same is true as a player. You're going to listen to other players who have been successful and have performed well. You either want to follow their example or learn something from them.

A player said something to me the other day about a young quarterback, and I remember what Coach Parcells used to say and it was so true. He'd say, "Don't tell me that you can do it. Show me you can do it." In other words, before you can be a leader, you've got to show people that you can accomplish these things. And Coach Parcells would say, "You don't have any pelts yet." And you'd wonder what he was talking about. And he'd say, "Well, you're like a fur trapper. Don't tell me how good a fur trapper you are if I walk outside and look at your horse and there are no furs on it. You got no pelts." His attitude was, once you've got some pelts, once you accomplish something on the field, then you will have the opportunity to be a leader.

Then it's up to you to use that opportunity. Remember the premise of this whole book. How do you achieve success as a quarterback? You begin by doing all the little things right: working hard at your drills, practicing, and learning the proper

game day

THE QUARTERBACK'S ROLE

I think the quarterback's main job is to get his team into the end zone, to score points. I always told Phil that his main responsibility was to engineer and conduct the team down the field, both running and passing, and get his team into the end zone. That's basically all I expect from the quarterback.

Leadership skills are important to do that, but as for the task itself, that's what I think his mission is. I've never been a coach that's too interested in passing stats, touchdown passes, percentages of completion, or any of that. When all was said and done there was only one question to be answered. Did his team score enough to win?

—**Bill Parcells**
Former Head Coach, New York Giants
Head Coach, New England Patriots

---

mechanics to help you perform at a higher level. And as you perform better, the effectiveness of your leadership will grow. Your teammates will listen to what you have to say. And then you can have an influence on your football team as a quarterback. You set the tone for your teammates. Do you want them to be quiet and reserved? Or do you want them to be loud and emotional? The quarterback can determine that. And he should be able to determine that because he's the one with the football. He calls the plays. He's publicly acknowledged as being the leader. The coaches acknowledge it all the time to the public and to the rest of the team even though they might not know they're doing it, because so much of the game centers on the quarterback.

LEADERSHIP

When I got to the Giants, Phil was in his sixth year and he really hadn't had that much playing time because of his injuries and all. So, when he really started to come on strong, he was already a five- or six-year veteran. And he had established himself as a professional quarterback and he knew what he was doing. There was never any doubt. Phil was a student of the game. We all knew he would take care of his job. And that made us all comfortable and more settled down and more focused on what we had to do. There wasn't a lot of thinking about what everyone else was going to do. We never worried especially about Phil. He set the tone. He set the example. And the rest of us studied and knew what we had to do because of what we saw him do.

–Mark Bavaro
Tight End, New York Giants
1985–1990

game day

The quarterback can have a bigger influence on the team than anybody except the head coach. The game is getting more and more focused on the quarterback because of the importance of the passing attack. So he has a lot of opportunities to do a lot for the team. And I'm not just talking about when he's on the field. The way he conducts himself off the field, the way he works in the weight room, the way he pays attention in team meetings—all those little things are just as important. That's leadership: doing all the little things right.

LEADERSHIP

In the quarterback position, you have to instill confidence in the rest of the players. It goes with the territory. It goes with the position. As the quarterback, you are the leader of the team. And as you go, the team goes. I don't think there's ever been a Super Bowl team or a very successful team where the quarterback has been an average player. I even look to our Super Bowl in 1990, when Jeff Hostetler was quarterbacking. Phil had taken the team through a very successful season and we had a great record. And then Jeff came in and showed that he was a great quarterback too.

—Bart Oates
Center, San Francisco 49ers

We've talked about the way improving your mechanics can make the difference in a game, in one or two critical plays. We've talked about the need to improve your skills. That's what helps the team when you get back together again in camp and begin the next season. When you use the off-time to enhance your mechanics, your conditioning, your speed, your strength...it will enhance the overall level of play for your team. That's why you work on your mechanics in the off-season. When you enhance your own skills, you enhance the overall skills of the team. That's very important. Take the initiative, exercise the discipline to make yourself better. Then when you get together again in camp, work with your teammates to become a precision unit.

SUCCESS

You love to go into a game with a guy like Phil Simms. He was the kind of guy who was going to do whatever it took to be successful. He was going to give you a hundred percent. And if it meant that he was going to take some physical punishment, it just didn't matter to him. You really appreciated the guy for his efforts. You appreciated that he had confidence in that position; knowing that he would make the big plays when you had to have them.

—Bart Oates
Center, San Francisco 49ers

game day

LEADERSHIP: I think that the number one thing you need to be a successful quarterback today is to be a leader. You must be able to get the team to follow you. You could go so far as to say that the guys around you should play at a higher level just because you're there. That's what a leader is. And that entails an awful lot of things: your preparation during the off-season, your preparation during the season, your toughness, your ability to react to adversity. All of those things are part of leadership. Being able to perform in a clutch situation will, of course, help you. A coach obviously wants a person like that to be the quarterback. He wants a leader, if at all possible. He's the guy who has to be consistently effective if you're going to win. I believe this is true at every level of the game. It doesn't make one bit of difference whether it's junior recreation football, high school, college, or the pros.

For you to win, one of two things has to happen: Either your quarterback has to produce and consistently be a winning influence on the team, or you must be dominant in every other phase of the game. There are very few exceptions where you can win without an effective quarterback. There have been a few, but if you really examine them, you will see that the team had an absolute, dominate, killer defense and a great running game. I mean everything else on the team has to be better than the other guy for you to win without an effective quarterback. The way the game of football is played today, if your quarterback doesn't produce, you don't win—on any level

For example, let's say you're down to the last two minutes of a game and you have the ball; you need someone who can lead your team down the field and get you what you need to win. That could be a long drive for a touchdown or it could be an extended final possession to maintain a lead. An effective quarterback is going to be able to do that for you. He won't do it every time but he should be able get some of them for you. That final drive may consist of eight running plays and only two passes but you know that he'll hit those two. Either you score or you keep the drive going so long that the other offense never gets a chance to get back on the field. You run the clock out. In the clutch times, it may only be a five-yard pass, but if it's third and four, a five-yard pass is a real important play. It could win the game. That's what your quarterback has to be able to do for you.

—George Henshaw
Offensive Coordinator, New York Giants

game day

CHAPTER 9

The Ball Never Lies (Diagnostic Chart)

Problem	Causes	Solutions	Page
Dropped snaps	Hand separation	Thumb-side-to-thumb-side hand position Bottom-hand pressure	34
Slow coming off line for drops	False stepping	Pigeon-toed stance under center	26
Fumbles	Carrying the ball with one hand	Two hands on the ball Front-hand pressure	35 40
Slipping	Rushing drops–leaning forward and stepping back too far on last step to stop momentum	Keep hips and shoulders level Don't overstep to land Don't lean too far forward to stop momentum away from line	49 54
Throwing low and short	Locking out front knee Landing on front foot toe-heel	Keep hips and shoulders level Land on front foot heel-toe Slightly bend both knees	88
Throwing high	Hips get out in front Back shoulder drops Front shoulder pitches up Throwing elbow drops	Keep hips and shoulders level Drop front shoulder slightly Look at target	89
Ducks and Helicopters	Hips get out in front Can't generate power Manipulating ball with hand to compensate Finish palm up No follow-through	Go back to proper sequence Complete follow-through with hand, thumb down	86
Late passing on sprint-outs	Strides too long on down portion of sprint	Shorten stride to chop steps Rise up slightly Cock ball to ear hole of helmet Dart-like throwing motion	122

Problem	Causes	Solutions	Page
Sore arm and shoulder	Grip too tight	Loosen grip Gap between palm and hand Strengthen arm	65
	Finger position on ball	If little finger is under laces move it to over the laces	64
	Arm throwing	Gain forward body momentum Push off back foot Rotate hips Drive nonthrowing elbow down and back Rotate shoulders, throwing arm, and ball leg	81
	Arm too tight	Keep arm loose and relaxed so it can whip through motion	85
Throwing behind receivers on crossing routes and slants	Stepping at or behind receiver with front foot	Step to where you expect receiver to be when you want him to catch it	121
Long passes tail out and fall short	Overstriding on front step so that your weight doesn't get over to your front foot on the follow-through	Shorten your stride Push off your back foot Throw your upper body over your front foot just ahead of the throw	90
Ball slips out of hand in wet weather	Squeezing ball too hard	Softer grip Slow down throwing motion Emphasize strong mechanics	195

the ball never lies